Take My Hand

Take My Hand

A Hope for Humanity

Mychelle Simms

XULON PRESS

Xulon Press
2301 Lucien Way #415
Maitland, FL 32751
407.339.4217
www.xulonpress.com

Paperback ISBN-: 978-1-66287-068-2
Ebook ISBN: 978-1-66287-069-9

The Tree

Whenever you feel
Like everything is falling apart,
Remember, trees have leaves,
and those leaves fall off.
Or, a strong gust of wind blows those leaves away.
Yet despite all of that, a tree stands tall in the wind
And understands some leaves will be lost,
but better days are to come.
And with that understanding,
New leaves are bound to grow.

Garret Simms
Son of the Author
West Texas A&M student

An Introduction

L ife is full of ups and downs, victories and defeats, lessons, and devastation. People are difficult, and relationships are hard. Mistakes can be life lessons or catastrophic events, which change a person forever. Humanity in itself is a broken system. People want to be loved, accepted, included, and forgiven. Many people today choose to walk a path without God. Many people live a life of fillers to keep their heads above water, people in their lives, food on the table, and money in their pockets; fillers that dissolve and erode. Experience and questions without answers or reasons leave people feeling hopeless. It is understandable that people are upset, full of fear and rejection, searching for truth, and in difficult battles. We all need love, support from other people, and a place to call home. Habits can be hard to establish and even more difficult to break. The mind will wander everywhere; it will search to quench a thirst that cannot find a drink. Is there hope for this broken life?

There is hope; he is a person, and his name is Jesus. He is the first and the last, the beginning and the end, the Alpha and Omega. He is omnipresent, almighty, and loves you beyond reason. He knows everything about you; he will forgive and redeem you. He can change everything. There is nothing too disappointing, awful, or frightening he fears. He won't back down and won't leave you. He can be your best friend.

As you turn the pages of this book, you will read stories of Jesus. You will see him move in a life no different than yours. You will see a connection and peace. He means what he says, and he says what he means. Even though you may not physically see him, you can know he is present. The Holy Spirit will come to live inside you, and you will never be alone. There isn't a special program you have to pass or a surgery you need. If you hand your life to Jesus and the Holy Spirit, they will do the work for you. You can live a life you have always wanted. There is hope. Turn the page.

Table of Contents

John 16:13

But when the friend comes, the Spirit of Truth, he will take you by the hand and guide you into all truth.

If we firmly grasp the Lord's hand, we will overcome fear. The Lord will never let go. The world will fall apart. But those of us holding the Lord's hand never will.

1

"Darkness cannot drive out darkness; only light can do that. Hate cannot drive out hate; only love can do that."
—*Martin Luther King Jr.*[1]

So Will I

May I Introduce You to My Father?

Focus: My Understanding is incomplete.

Scripture: My understanding is incomplete now, but one day I will understand everything, just as everything about me has been fully understood. Until then, there are three things that remain: faith, hope, and love—yet love surpasses them all (1 Cor. 13:12–13).

W hat happens when things don't go as you planned? Does God still love you then? Does God sit with you in dark times? I know God doesn't love me more today than he did yesterday, but I truly think in dark times, somehow, he gives more of himself to me. He doesn't change how he loves. He simply shows more of himself to me. I know what darkness feels like. I know the warmth of God's love in the middle of the darkness.

When I was around twenty-five, my mom found out she had a rare blood disorder called polycythemia vera. It is similar to Leukemia. Polycythemia vera is a rare, chronic blood cancer where the bone marrow produces too many red blood cells. Too many red blood cells can cause the blood to thicken. Thicker blood doesn't flow normally through arteries and veins. Increased blood thickness and decreased blood flow, as well as abnormalities in platelets and white blood cells, may increase the risk of blood clots. As the disease develops, it takes an effect on daily life and begins to cause issues within the body's organs. Over time, my sweet mom began to get sicker and sicker.

I began to study and seek God for my mom's healing. I was certain she would live through the disease. My mom's sickness drew me closer to the Lord. On February 24, 2001, I received a call from my dad. He said that mom fell during the night or early morning. She had hit her head on the nightstand (my parents did not sleep in the same room due to my mom's condition). When he woke up, he found her lying on the floor. She was being transported to a hospital in Lubbock, but the prognosis was not good. My sisters lived in Oklahoma and Dallas. It would be a while before they could return home. Mitch, my husband, and I headed to Lubbock.

When we arrived and I saw her, I was scared. I had never seen a person so close to death. We had recently buried my husband's mom in January of the same year, and this was more than I could handle. I stood in the emergency room looking at Mom and knowing she was hurt. Her brain was swelling, and they were going to perform emergency surgery. I have never agonized like that. At that moment, I was angry, very angry. I was scared and confused. This is not what I had prayed for.

Many things can happen during times like these. Your mind can think horrible thoughts. Your tongue can yell terrible things. Your body can kick and punch. I was a young Christian at the time. I was beginning to understand authority, Scripture, and the accuser, but I was uncertain. I didn't believe what my eyes were seeing, and I didn't believe the lies of the accuser, but the doctors were not positive. They began to tell us to make arrangements for her. My dad and I had difficult decisions to make. By the time she came out of surgery, my sisters were home. I still remember picking them up at the airport. I don't think I will ever forget my day of sadness in everyone else's normal life. I can still see them coming off the planes with such hurt and fear in their eyes.

Over the next four days, we encountered Satan like never before. His hatred for us was loud and in our faces. He came to kill my mom. He came to destroy my family. We didn't eat much. We didn't sleep much. We didn't laugh much. My mom's family came to the hospital. My grandparents were heartbroken. Death was ever present. My dad, my husband, my Uncle Ed, and my sisters refused to believe the lies. I learned to completely rely on God. We went into Mom's room every time they would let us in. We were allowed to see her around four times a day. In her room, we prayed. We prayed like never before. We believed she would walk out of the room. She never did.

You may wonder how this story can show the love of God. Why would you share this story if you are trying to get me to trust this God of yours? Your mom died, and you love God even more? I don't understand that. If that is what you are thinking, I understand your point. I am not going to say I don't miss her.

I am not going to say I don't cry. It has been twenty-one years, and I miss my mom every day. I wish she was here. However, I have never been mad at God for taking my mom home. I can honestly say those words and mean them. I know God. He is my father. I want you to know him too.

You see, through praying and fasting, God's love for our family was intense. He didn't leave us. He didn't leave my mom. He gave her a choice. She chose to be with him. He always gives us a choice. From the beginning, God wanted to love us and wanted us to love him back. My mom did love him. She was ready to go home for eternity. God didn't kill her, and he didn't take her away from me. She simply made a choice to live in heaven. I was given a glimpse of my mom on her final day on earth. I saw her take the hand of Jesus. She is beautiful; no more sickness, no more failing body, just peace and glow. She is happy. I will see her again.

Hillsong United, one of my favorite worship groups, writes God's love for us like no other group. I absolutely love them. This is part of a song entitled, "So Will I (100 Billion X)." It is a great way to wake up and hand my day over to the Creator! I suggest you look it up and listen to it.

So Will I by Hillsong United[2]

God of creation
There at the start
Before the beginning of time
With no point of reference
You spoke to the dark
And fleshed out the wonder of light
And as You speak

A hundred billion galaxies are born
In the vapor of Your breath the planets form
If the stars were made to worship so will I
I can see Your heart in everything You've made
Every burning star
A signal fire of grace
If creation sings Your praises so will I

It is a challenge sometimes to understand the magnitude of the God of creation. This song helps me recall just how BIG and majestic God is. This chapter reflects one idea or question, "How can I write down your love for us, Lord? How can I possibly explain what you mean to me so that others can fully understand?" You see, I know the amazing love of the Father, Son, and Holy Spirit because I have experience with them. I have grown up with them. I know them. From the time I could talk and understand, my life angel, my mom, taught me about this amazing person named Jesus. I was immersed in Bible stories, Sunday school, and Girls in Action (GA's). My grandfather was a deacon at First Baptist Church, sang in the choir, and served on the board. Servanthood was a way of life. If it was Sunday, I was in church.

As I grew up, God became more personal to me. He was present, and I heard his voice. However, I stiffed-armed him at times when it wasn't "cool" to be Christian. I made choices to leave him out of my life, especially at the end of high school and my early college years. He never left me. I went through a rebellious stage and partied, drank, and stayed out too late, but there was always a hand on my life.

Eventually, I got married, and Mitch and I became members of Faith Christian Family Church in Clovis, New Mexico.

We have been members ever since, for over twenty-five years. Under the church's leadership, we have grown and watched the Holy Spirit move in our lives. We have two boys; Paden is twenty-four, and Garret is twenty. They both love God and see in the spirit. We learn from them as much as they learn from us. We have our share of disappointments, wrong decisions, heartache, death, and accidents, but through it all, God.

It is my heart's desire to reach my arm out through this book to those of you who simply do not understand this love.

Maybe, you've never wanted God or never been introduced to him. Or maybe you knew him once, and then the accuser came and hurt you and blamed it on God. Maybe you have never felt or known love. Please take some time to let me introduce you to my Father. No matter what type of relationship you have with your earthly parents, there is a heavenly Father that is all about you. God, the creator, is God, our father.

For a moment, let's go back in time before the dawn of creation. Let's take a look at the beginning. In the first part of the lyrics, "So Will I Hillsong United,"[3] the song discusses the amazing love of God for us. *"God of creation, there at the start, before the beginning of time, with no point of reference, you spoke to the dark, and fleshed out the wonder of light."* Can you imagine what it must have been like at the beginning of time? I have given it some thought, and here are my ideas.

God sat in his heavens as the eternal clock maker. King of all, with a few words, he set the stars in motion and formed the depth of the universe. He sat and dreamed. He envisioned a people. He dreamed of you, his cherished aspiration. He dreamed of me. He set forth ideas and images of every family member. He considered everyone you love. His ambition was to create a people he could have relationships with. To begin, he needed to create a home for them, a place of perfect balance and tranquility.

"First this: God created the Heavens and Earth—All you see and don't see. Earth was a soup of nothingness, a bottomless emptiness, an inky blackness, God's spirit brooded like a bird above the watery abyss." "God spoke: 'Light!' And light appeared. God saw that light was good and separated light from dark. God named the light Day, he named the dark Night. It was evening. It was morning—Day One." Genesis. 1:1-5 Message

The word *spoke* means to express thoughts, feelings, or opinions orally.[4] Take, for a moment, what happened when God spoke. His natural sound, a voice like thunder, declared his thoughts. As this occurred, the soup of nothingness became light. It is important to grasp the meaning of God's authority and ability from the beginning of time. I believe this is the foundation of all that exists. If we don't recognize the power of God to pronounce, declare, and create, then why believe the Bible? We must accept as truth that God's words change the atmosphere. His words address the sum of what is important because it all relates back to him. God's words change the atmosphere to the extent that his Word changes dark into light. He can change your dark situations into light if you will speak his Word. He wants to change your atmosphere; just ask him to.

"God spoke: 'Sky! In the middle of the waters, separate water from water!' God made the sky. He separated the water under the sky from the water above the sky. And there it was: He named the sky the Heavens; It was evening. It is morning—Day Two." Genesis. 1:6-8 Message

God began to form the earth. He carefully thought about the balance needed for humans to live supernatural lives. He considered the water, mountains, and light and darkness. He created the earth full of color, texture, smell, sound, and beauty. His human creation would always have something beautiful to gaze upon. He developed every flower, pedal, tree, rock, and droplet of water. He created sound and smell. He created food.

Genesis. 1:11–13 Message
God spoke: "Earth, green up! Grow all varieties of seed-bearing plants, every sort of fruit bearing tree." And there it was. Earth produced green seed-bearing plants, all varieties, and fruit-bearing trees of all sorts. God saw that it was good
It was evening. It was morning—Day Three.

God's voice created his desires. Whatever he speaks comes into existence. Whatever we speak, according to Scripture, using the name of Jesus, comes into existence. Understanding the power of our confession aloud based on Scripture is essential to a victorious life. The power of the tongue is stronger than we consider. God left nothing undone. Yes, man, his beloved creation, would have every necessity because God loved him with all of his heart.

Genesis. 1:20–23 Message
God spoke: "Swarm, Ocean, with fish and all sea life!
Birds fly through the sky over Earth!" God created the
huge whales, all the swarms of life in the waters, and every
species of flying birds. God saw that it was good. God
blessed them: "Prosper! Reproduce! Fill the Ocean! Birds,
reproduce on Earth!"
It was evening. It was morning—Day Five.

All was set to introduce man to the Lord's creation, for this raw, human man would be of the purest form, clean and unblended. He would be natural and full of hope and joy. God adored man.

Genesis. 1:26–28: Message
God spoke: "Let us make human beings in our image,
make them reflecting our nature, so they can be respon-
sible for the fish in the sea, the birds in the air, the cattle,
and yes, for the Earth itself and every animal that moves
on the face of the Earth." God created human beings; He
created them godlike; reflecting God's nature. He cre-
ated them male and female. God blessed them: "Prosper!
Reproduce! Fill Earth! Take charge! Be responsible for the
fish in the sea and birds in the air, for every living thing
that moves on the face of the Earth." Then God said: "I've
given you every sort of seed-bearing plant on Earth, and
every kind of fruit-bearing tree, given them to you for
food. To all animals and all birds, everything that moves
and breathes, I give whatever grows out of the ground for
food." And there it was.

God created man, you, and me, to be responsible for the earth. He placed his nature in us. We were to represent God's inherent character. God was the controlling force in the universe, and he handed the control over to man. He continually spoke of the good, prosperity, reproduction, and ownership of all he created. The Lord handed over his planet to man out of love. He wanted us to enjoy our new home. He was eager to bond with us.

Our Father thought about us and created a planet. He created a planet for our occupation. He created a place for us to live and prosper. Your daddy gave you a planet. He designed food and fish and animals for you. He didn't create a system of exchange or barter. He didn't make us go to work for a wage. Money is a man-made system. He loved us so much that he made a planet for us. I am in awe when I consider that he gave us a planet. He was so meticulous in forming it. He spared nothing, and it was perfect. He created you and me from his own image. He wanted us to share in his glory and beauty. Why? LOVE! God wanted to feast and fellowship with us. God prepared a table for the newly created man. He gave him a home. He gave him a universe. He gave him life. He gave him a companion, all because God is LOVE!

Soon after man was walking on earth, God realized he wasn't as happy as he hoped he would be. You see, God gave man free choice. He wanted this raw, unblended man, Adam, to want to choose him. Adam did choose God and talked with him daily. But something was missing. Adam needed his own friend. So out of God's love for Adam, he created Eve. God put Adam to sleep and took one of his ribs to make a woman. The woman was called Eve. *Genesis. 2:18–22: Message: "God said, 'It is not good for the Man to be alone, I'll make him a helper, a* companion."' *"God put the man into a deep sleep. As he slept, he removed one of his ribs and replaced it with flesh. God then used the rib that he had taken from the Man to make Woman and presented her to the Man."*

Out of God's unselfish love for man, he created a woman to walk the earth with him. God was pleased that Eve made Adam so happy. They walked, talked, and explored together. They enjoyed each other physically and mentally. All was good on earth. God's great love for us created love in us.

LOVE, love, love; God is love. Love*(s)* is a strong affection for another arising out of kinship or personal ties, devotion.[1] God's love for us is like a gigantic hole ready to swallow us up. He created us in his image and then gave us free will. Why? He loves us. God loved us so much that he gave us the option to love him back. We still have that choice today. God only wants our love back. I believe he needed someone to lavish his goodness upon. If everything, including the stars, belonged to you, might you want someone to share it with? God is! God creates! God owns! So if *all* is yours, wouldn't you want someone to share it with? I wish I sometimes could get out of my own way and let God adore me and simply love him back. I need to allow him to completely restore my heart to his original intent for me. *"Truly the joy of the Lord is my strength"* (Nehemiah. 8:10) Message.

Unfortunately, the word love has lost some of its meaning. The word is thrown around without time to consider its worth and value. You see, when God was preparing his earth for us, it was with complete and total endearment. We are the darling

---

[1] Webster's 1828 American Dictionary of the English Language, Walking Lion Press, West Valley City, UT, 2010.

of his eye, his kingdom seekers, his prized possession. Out of adoration, he created male and female. The words "in the beginning," are of such magnitude but often just read over. I don't think we understand the depth of God's benevolence. I think we have dulled down the word love until it has lost some of its sparkle. Have we reduced God's love and our walk with others to a clanging cymbal? Has it been reduced to a symbol of "pie in the sky" that is truly a bunch of noise? (See 1 Cor. 13:1.)

We say we love, but by what means of motivation. Would you buy the most expensive meat, wine, or gifts every time your family comes over for dinner just so they were happy? Would you share beautiful art or keep exotic animals in the backyard just for their pleasure? God did just that. According to 1 Corinthians 13:4–8: *Message*

Love is large and incredibly patient. Love is gentle and consistently kind to all. It refuses to be jealous when blessing comes to someone else. Love does not brag about one's achievements nor inflate its own importance. Love does not traffic in shame and disrespect, nor selfishly seek its own honor. Love is not easily irritated or quick to take offense. Love joyfully celebrates honesty and finds no delight in what is wrong. Love is a safe place of shelter, for it never stops believing the best for others. Love never takes failure as defeat, for it never gives up.

Let's take a few minutes and replace the word love with God. God is love. Our Father is all the Scripture describes as love. "*Love is large and incredibly patient. Love is gentle and consistently kind to all.*" Your father, God, is large and incredibly patient. He is gentle and kind. He picks us up when we stumble.

He dusts us off when we make mistakes. He smiles at us and talks with us. He forgives quickly. He teaches us.

"Love does not traffic in shame and disrespect, nor selfishly seek its own honor." God does not traffic our shame. He doesn't put it on social media for the world to see. He doesn't humiliate. He doesn't broadcast your sin to the world. He doesn't condemn. He covers our sin through the blood of Jesus. He forgives us and welcomes us into our rightful place. God doesn't force you to love him. He wants our hearts to be freely given to him. He will not seek his own honor in your life.

"Love is not easily irritated or quick to take offense."

God isn't in heaven waiting to catch you in sin. He isn't trying to make you fall. He isn't filling your life with rules and regulations so he can punish you. All his promises are yes and amen. All the rules he places in front us are for our own good. He isn't mad at the decision you made yesterday. He doesn't hold grudges. He is patient. He is long-suffering. He will help you through any situation. In our society today, if you disagree with a person's perspective, he or she may become offended. They may cut you out of their lives. They may "unfriend" you. They may even turn their back on you. Our Father in heaven will not do that. He will not turn his back on you. He will ask you to stop sinning and turn toward him, but he will not "unfriend" you!

"Love is a safe place of shelter, for it never stops believing the best for others. Love never takes failure as defeat, for it never gives up." God is a safe place of shelter. God is my shelter. God is my home. God is my safety. God is my refuge. God wants me safe from harm. God wants me to run to him. He never stops believing the best for me. He always gives me a second chance.

He is always with me. He never gives up on me. He forgives, and then He forgives again. He sees my potential. He knows my heart. He stands me up and gives me protection. He teaches me to be strong. He gives me his Word to speak. He gives me keys to things on heaven and earth. He places his armor on me. He calls me child, royalty, and a soldier in his army. He goes before me. He sees today, yesterday, and forever. He formed me in my mother's womb. He knows every hair on my head. He is my all in all. God will never give up on me or you! Ever!

Life isn't easy. The accuser hates us. To hurt us is to hurt God, and he takes pleasure in hurting God. He doesn't get to be loved by God anymore. Love has been taken from him. I will explain who the accuser is in more depth later. You need to understand who he is and what he does. But for now, I invite you to stop and get quiet. Please ask God to come into the situations of your life and love you. He will be honored to do so.

1 Corinthians 13:8: Message
Love never stops loving. It extends beyond the gift of prophecy, which eventually fades away. It is more enduring than tongues, which will one day fall silent. Love remains long after words of knowledge are forgotten. Our present knowledge and our prophecies are but partial, but when love's perfection arrives, the partial will fade away."

Remember, God is love. God never stops loving. God never fades away. God is enduring. He remains long after life on earth is over. We know partially, but God knows all.

He created a planet for you. He made you out of his own image. You are his child. Come and experience the love of our real Father!

We have been introduced to a supreme being, a supreme being who lives in the heavens. I know it is hard to understand the love of a God you have never seen. I simply ask that you find a quiet space and ask God to talk to you. The search for love can be over if you will just slow your mind, get quiet, and just ask him to come into your heart. When you call out to the Lord with a sincere heart, he will meet you. You will know he is with you. I cannot convince you that there is a God. All I can do is present an understanding that there is a love so great that it will swallow you and all of your mistakes. It will pull you out of any pit. It will wash you clean and provide courage to start fresh. I am not special. I am not more worthy. I simply said yes. Take my hand.

Try It:

1. Go for a walk and ask Jesus to join you.
2. Listen to "So Will I" by Hillsong United.
3. Give God a chance to introduce himself to you.

Scripture: "My understanding is incomplete now, but one day I will understand everything, just as everything about me has been fully understood. Until then, there are three things that remain: faith, hope, and love—yet love surpasses them all (1 Cor. 13:12–13).

2

"A child is an uncut diamond." —Austin O Malley [5]

On His Shoulders

Who Are You Dependent On?

Focus: We grow up spiritually by becoming a child of God.

Scripture: These words I speak to you are not incidental additions to your life, homeowner improvements to your standard of living. They are foundational words, words to build a life on. Matthew 7:24

It is summertime, and out in the front yard, a little girl twirls in circles, singing. Her beautiful blond hair and emerald-green eyes are alive. She is happy. Unaware that anyone is watching her, she sings and picks daisies from the grass. She giggles and sings some more. From down deep in her heart springs forth a joy that is pure, almost golden. She has a happiness that is unlike any other. She has a joy that isn't from this world. She sings and plays.

Children often have a spirit that is difficult to define. But some of them are more than happy; they seem to live life on another level. They own a purity of heart that seeps into anyone around them. They move with a love that is unconditional and very real. In fact, this love is so pure that it will love without worry, forgive without hesitation, and reunite broken souls without knowing. There is no fear in little ones like this. They believe and trust, look through your soul, and help you become a better person.

As I walk out the trailer door, this beautiful angel turns and looks at me. She yells, "Good morning, Aunt Shell," and brings me the daisies she has collected. I am almost in tears as this beautiful little girl meets me with hugs and kisses. "Did you see how pretty the sun was this morning?" she asks. "Watch this," she smiles as she flips through the yard. I have often said that if we could bottle up what is inside of Mia and sell it, we would all be very rich. In my heart, I pray, "Lord always allow our Mia to never change. Keep her safe and watch over her. Lord, thank you for this precious little girl."

I wonder where that little girl once inside of me has gone. It seems like a lifetime ago when I was that happy and carefree. Every time I have the honor of being with Mia Grace, I am a happier person. Her squeaky voice makes me smile, and her laugh is one in a million. She always sees the good in everything. She lives life and doesn't waste her time. At nine years old, she has life under control better than most adults. What makes her spirit so sure and content?

Child faith. Growing up is difficult. We all go through times in our lives when we are unsure of ourselves. We learn to cope with stress. Sometimes we don't cope well at all. As we grow up, pressures of this world can become overwhelming, and sometimes we lose the inner child that is so essential to our lives. Unfortunately, some of us have never had a childhood, which can be very difficult to overcome. The child in all of us is essential for a healthy adulthood.

I believe this is why the Lord called David a child after his own heart. It is also why Jesus rarely addressed God as God but as Father. The Lord never intended for us to push through our own lives. His purpose was for us to trust him with everything. Lean not unto our own understanding but believe and trust in him. Trust.

Trust is a big word. Trust can be a difficult word or the best word. Trust(s) is defined by as a firm belief in the reliability, truth, ability or strength of someone or something.[2] Our father, God, wants to have a firm belief in his reliability.

In my life, I have either trusted God completely, or I don't trust him at all. I have had a false sense of responsibility that has plagued my life with anxiety. I have suffered from horrible panic attacks and worry. I have hated myself and not allowed myself to be free. I have carried financial debt on my shoulders like a weighted vest. I have feared lack, and I have a difficult time with resting. It is a scary place to be.

Placing my trust in a source that I cannot physically see is difficult in certain areas. I am grateful that God understands my soul, and he works with me to change my thinking. He loves me with unconditional love and wants me to be happy. He is my father. My work is to become a child again. I should sing rather than cry, trust rather than worry, and listen rather than reason. He will show me how to move and when to stay still;

---

[2] Webster's 1828 American Dictionary of the English Language, Walking Lion Press, West Valley City, UT, 2010.

he will cause my path to be straight. I have to learn to become a child again and ask my Father to take care of me and be certain that he will.

If I were allowed one day with Jesus, what would that day look like? I think I would want to sit and just listen to him. I would want him to talk and allow him the time he needed to teach me what I need to know. I have the Bible to rely on, but at times I think I try to reason as a scholar rather than trust as a child. There is a series called *The Chosen*, which I highly recommend watching. It ties Jesus to common people and shows the relationship and concern he has for each individual life. It helps me understand how normal Jesus is and how my concerns are his.

In John 8:23, Jesus said, *"You're tied down to the mundane; I'm in touch with what is beyond your horizons. You live in terms of what you see and touch. I'm living on other terms."*

In Matthew 7:24–27, Jesus said:

These words I speak to you are not incidental additions to your life, homeowner improvements to your standard of living. They are foundational words, words to build a life on. If you work these words into your life, you are like a smart carpenter who built his house on solid rock. Rain poured down, the river flooded, a tornado hit—but nothing moved that house. It was fixed to the rock. But if you just use my words in Bible studies and don't work them into your life, you are like a stupid carpenter who built his house on the sandy beach. When a storm rolled in and the waves came up, it collapsed like a house of cards.

The title of this chapter is "On His Shoulders." I can remember when both of my boys were younger, their favorite place was on the shoulders of my husband, especially when they were tired. Mitch would place them on his shoulders and carry them around for miles. He never seemed to tire of it, even when they drooled on his head. He was a dad, and this is what a dad does. He carries his children when they are too tired to carry themselves. He carries his children when they don't know the way. He carries his children to get them somewhere they need to go. He carries his children simply out of love for their well-being. I can remember them slumped over from exhaustion from the day; so tired they couldn't move, couldn't carry themselves, couldn't be independent of him. There wasn't a choice; Mitch picked them up, and he never complained.

When we are placed on the shoulders of our Father, our perspective changes. What we see changes. Our safety changes. We become attached to the person who carries us. Our bodies no longer move and direct; something much greater carries us where we need to go. How long has it been since you climbed on the shoulders of your dad? Now that you are grown and responsible. Now that others depend on you? How long has it been since you were a child? How long has it been since you asked God to carry you? Jesus wants us to consider what he said, *"These words I speak to you are not incidental additions to your life, homeowner improvements to your standard of living. They are foundational words, words to build a life on. If you work these words into your life, you are like a smart carpenter who built his house on solid rock."* These are foundational words to build a life on, no matter the situation; to work into our lives; that change the way we live; and that give us courage to trust him with everything.

Child faith is a faith influenced by the environment of God's heart. Childlike faith is a young one with little experience, one hundred percent dependent on the Father. As the child feels more loved and accepted, the view of the child changes. God, on the other hand, lifts the child up and securely places her on his shoulders. He is happy to do it. In fact, it gives him great satisfaction to be the protector, deliverer, teacher, and hope of this child. The cool thing is that he is the father for every single one of us.

God carries his children when they are too tired to carry themselves. The happiness and triumph of the Lord is my physical strength to withstand great force or pressure. The child of faith can give the assuring confession that heavenly promises are no idle dreams, no "perhaps." He rests upon the divine promises that cannot fail. His deeds match his declarations. God is obligated by his character to fulfill it, which he did. Human promises are not binding regarding impossibilities. But to God, a promise is sure of performance. Bill Johnson paraphrased.

In Luke 10, there is a story dear to my heart, a story of two sisters, two sisters with the same invitation to sit with Jesus; two sisters with different perspectives: one to serve, the other to listen. Beginning in verse 38, the story is as follows:

> As they continued their travel, Jesus entered a village. A woman by the name of Martha welcomed him and made him feel quite at home. She had a sister, Mary, who sat before the Master, hanging on every word he said. But Martha was pulled away by all she had to do in the kitchen. Later, she stepped in, interrupting them. "Master, don't you care that my sister has abandoned the kitchen to me? Tell her to lend me a hand." The Master

*said, "Martha, dear Martha, you're fussing far too much
and getting yourself worked up over nothing. One thing
only is essential, and Mary has chosen it—it's the main
course and won't be taken from her."*

The question is, which sister are you? Whether male or
female, which perspective do you view life from? Are you the
worker or the listener? Are you so busy that you never take time
to listen and make sure your business is lining up with God's
voice in your life? Do you take the time to ask him before you
just work another day away? I wonder what Jesus was teaching
at the time. He must have been explaining something of importance, as he clearly stated that Mary was learning what she
needed to know. Consider, Jesus was in this house, and one
sister decided to listen while the other needed a clean kitchen.
There was a time in my life that I would have been in the kitchen
with Martha complaining about my sister.

I am sure those of us who are Christians can read this story
and realize an opportunity missed by Martha. We can look back
and think, *Man, didn't you realize who was in your living room,
teaching?* It might be easy to judge Martha for not spending
quality time with the Savior of the world. However, don't we
do the same every day? And honestly, maybe even worse, as we
always have the Holy Spirit with us. Martha was sitting with the
human form of Jesus; we have the spirit of Jesus in us, ready to
consult with us on any issue. Do we listen? Or are we concerned
with dirty dishes, better known as the next task?

In your mind, you might be thinking, *Yeah, but don't the
dishes need to be cleaned up? Isn't it the responsible thing to do?
We must take care of what we are given.* Yes, we do need to be
responsible. But responsibility can become a yoke of bondage. It

is important to allow the Holy Spirit to teach you your boundaries. It is important to let him guide you in your perspective. While some of us work too much, others work too little, and both sides are not healthy. Healthiness comes from depending on the Holy Spirit to teach balance.

In my own life, I allowed human expectations to become what I thought were God's expectations. Due to this thought process, I put a lot of pressure on myself to not disappoint those around me. I didn't allow myself to make mistakes. I wasn't harsh on others for messing up, but I didn't give myself the same grace. Because of this mindset, I created wrong thought patterns that led to one path: work produces results. I must take care of myself and all of those I care about. Fear of money and lack were ever present in all the decisions I made.

I wish I could say I broke this cycle when I was young, but I didn't. I just added to my plate of responsibility until it broke. I had strongholds of misplaced responsibility and perfection to the point that I was angry most of the time. I was overly concerned with rejection. The fear of rejection created a workaholic mentality. Fear of not being enough, doing enough, prepping enough, writing enough, and being accountable created an overload of strain and pressure. Migraines, hormone imbalance, anger, and depression were all new residents in my life. Trust was absent. Work and performance became my focus.

So how do you switch from being overwhelming work minded to a resting and listening mentality? For me, I had a nervous breakdown. This is not a recommendation, but it happened to me. Stress, fear, and anger built up to the point that I completely broke. My Christian knowledge was no match for the demonic presence I had allowed in my life. I knew a lot of Scripture, but I didn't understand how much God loved me. I wasn't on God's shoulders; I was running in every direction, trying to fix everything. God was with me, but I sure wasn't letting him carry me anywhere. My house was built on sand.

Sometimes tears are the only solution. Sometimes we have to break in order to find our way home. I needed help, and this story helped to change my life. Mary just wanted to be with Jesus. Mary just sat and listened. Mary was learning how much Jesus and her Father loved her. Mary was eating the bread of life. Mary knew what was important and wasn't distracted. Lord, help me be like Mary. Help me see myself as you do! I need your shield and guidance. Help me change my mind! Help me, Lord, to sit and listen. Help me become a child again.

No matter what Jesus was teaching at the time, Mary was listening. Jesus's words fed her. She understood the words coming from Jesus were dipped in his honey of pure love. She knew that whatever he said to her would sustain her and help her with whatever she faced. She got it. She made time for him. She knew that to live tomorrow, she needed Jesus today. She was on the shoulders of Jesus. She knew he had her life in his hands, and she wasn't scared to climb up and let him take her places.

The more spiritually mature you are, the more you sit and listen to Jesus making yourself available to him. When you do this, you grow up because God now sees your spirit as a spirit after his own heart. God's heart is pure, just, and compassionate. It's how David became king. He was a man after God's own heart. It is a complete role reversal from what the world thinks.

David and Goliath is a story of child faith that won a nation to the Lord. Let's take a minute and visualize how David trusted God to destroy a giant standing in the way of Israel.

1 Samuel 17:1–58:

Now the Philistines gathered their forces for war and assembled at Sokoh in Judah. They pitched camp at Ephes Dammim, between Sokoh and Azekah. Saul and the Israelites assembled and camped in the Valley of Elah and drew up their battle line to meet the Philistines. The Philistines occupied one hill and the Israelites another, with the valley between them.

A champion named Goliath, who was from Gath, came out of the Philistine camp. His height was six cubits and a span. He had a bronze helmet on his head and wore a coat of scale armor of bronze weighing five thousand shekels; on his legs he wore bronze greaves, and a bronze javelin was slung on his back. His spear shaft was like a weaver's rod, and its iron point weighed six hundred shekels. His shield bearer went ahead of him.

Goliath stood and shouted to the ranks of Israel, "Why do you come out and line up for battle? Am I not a Philistine, and are you not the servants of Saul? Choose a man and have him come down to me. If he is able to fight and kill me, we will become your subjects; but if I overcome him and kill him, you will become our subjects and serve us." Then the Philistine said, "This day I defy the armies of Israel! Give me a man and let us fight each other." On hearing the Philistine's words, Saul and all the Israelites were dismayed and terrified.

Now David was the son of an Ephrathite named Jesse, who was from Bethlehem in Judah. Jesse had eight sons, and in Saul's time he was very old. Jesse's three oldest sons had followed Saul to the war: The firstborn was Eliab; the second, Abinadab; and the third, Shammah. David was the youngest. The three oldest followed Saul, but David went back and forth from Saul to tend his father's sheep at Bethlehem.

For forty days the Philistine came forward every morning and evening and took his stand.

Now Jesse said to his son David, "Take this ephah of roasted grain and these ten loaves of bread for your brothers and hurry to their camp. Take these ten cheeses to the commander of their unit. See how your brothers are and bring back some assurance-from them. They are with Saul and all the men of Israel in the Valley of Elah, fighting against the Philistines."

Early in the morning David left the flock in the care of a shepherd, loaded up and set out, as Jesse had directed. He reached the camp as the army was going out to its battle positions, shouting the war cry. Israel and the Philistines were drawing up their lines facing each other. David left his things with the keeper of supplies, ran to the battle lines and asked his brothers how they were. As he was talking with them, Goliath, the Philistine champion from Gath, stepped out from his lines and shouted his usual defiance, and David heard it. Whenever the Israelites saw the man, they all fled from him in great fear.

Now the Israelites had been saying, "Do you see how this man keeps coming out? He comes out to defy Israel. The king will give great wealth to the man who kills him. He will also give him his daughter in marriage and will exempt his family from taxes in Israel."

David asked the men standing near him, "What will be done for the man who kills this Philistine and removes this disgrace from Israel? Who is this uncircumcised Philistine that he should defy the armies of the living God?"

They repeated to him what they had been saying and told him, "This is what will be done for the man who kills him."

When Eliab, David's oldest brother, heard him speaking with the men, he burned with anger at him and asked, "Why have you come down here? And with whom did you leave those few sheep in the wilderness? I know how conceited you are and how wicked your heart is; you came down only to watch the battle."

"Now what have I done?" said David. "Can't I even speak?" He then turned away to someone else and brought up the same matter, and the men answered him as before. What David said was overheard and reported to Saul, and Saul sent for him.

David said to Saul, "Let no one lose heart on account of this Philistine; your servant will go and fight him."

Saul replied, "You are not able to go out against this Philistine and fight him; you are only a young man, and he has been a warrior from his youth."

But David said to Saul, "Your servant has been keeping his father's sheep. When a lion or a bear came and carried off a sheep from the flock, I went after it, struck it and rescued the sheep from its mouth. When it turned on me, I seized it by its hair, struck it and killed it. Your servant has killed both the lion and the bear; this uncircumcised Philistine will be like one of them, because he has defied the armies of the living God. The Lord who rescued me from the paw of the lion and the paw of the bear will rescue me from the hand of this Philistine."

Saul said to David, "Go, and the Lord be with you."

Then Saul dressed David in his own tunic. He put a coat of armor on him and a bronze helmet on his head. David fastened on his sword over the tunic and tried walking around, because he was not used to them.

"I cannot go in these," he said to Saul, "because I am not used to them." So, he took them off. Then he took his staff in his hand, chose five smooth stones from the stream, put them in the pouch of his shepherd's bag and, with his sling in his hand, approached the Philistine.

Meanwhile, the Philistine, with his shield bearer in front of him, kept coming closer to David. He looked David over and saw that he was little more than a boy, glowing with health and handsome, and he despised him. He said to David, "Am I a dog, that you come at me with sticks?" And the Philistine cursed David by his gods. "Come here," he said, "and I'll give your flesh to the birds and the wild animals!"

David said to the Philistine, "You come against me with sword and spear and javelin, but I come against you in the name of the Lord Almighty, the God of the armies of Israel, whom you have defied. This day the Lord will deliver you into my hands, and I'll strike you down and cut off your head. This very day I will give the carcasses of the Philistine army to the birds and the wild animals, and the whole world will know that there is a God in Israel. All those gathered here will know that it is not by sword or spear that the Lord saves; for the battle is the Lord's, and he will give all of you into our hands."

As the Philistine moved closer to attack him, David ran quickly toward the battle line to meet him. Reaching into his bag and taking out a stone, he slung it and struck the Philistine on the forehead. The stone sank into his forehead, and he fell facedown on the ground.

So David triumphed over the Philistine with a sling and a stone; without a sword in his hand he struck down the Philistine and killed him.

David ran and stood over him. He took hold of the Philistine's sword and drew it from the sheath. After he killed him, he cut off his head with the sword.

When the Philistines saw that their hero was dead, they turned and ran. Then the men of Israel and Judah surged forward with a shout and pursued the Philistines to the entrance of Gath[f] and to the gates of Ekron. Their dead were strewn along the Shaaraim road to Gath and Ekron. When the Israelites returned from chasing the Philistines, they plundered their camp.

David took the Philistine's head and brought it to Jerusalem; he put the Philistine's weapons in his own tent.

As Saul watched David going out to meet the Philistine, he said to Abner, commander of the army, "Abner, whose son is that young man?"

Abner replied, "As surely as you live, Your Majesty, I don't know."

The king said, "Find out whose son this young man is."

As soon as David returned from killing the Philistine, Abner took him and brought him before Saul, with David still holding the Philistine's head.

"Whose son are you, young man?" Saul asked him.

David said, "I am the son of your servant Jesse of Bethlehem."

We grow up when we depend more on the Lord. I grow up when I trust the Lord more. I learn to trust without fear, borders, anger, and what-ifs. To become a warrior for the Lord, like David, I must learn to be the shepherd boy first. Being mature is trusting God with your life, future, health, finances, family, or education. Complete trust casts out all fear. When you trust God and climb on his shoulders, your perspective changes. He has lifted you up above the mess and set you firmly on his body. His movement becomes your movement. He takes you where you are destined to go. He carries you there, and you are not worried about yourself because God takes you to your destination.

Therefore, the simplicity of Mary sitting at the feet of Jesus is far more mature than Martha and all her distractions of work.

For a minute, let's use our imagination and pretend that Jesus is in our living room, and he is teaching us. Proverbs 3:5–12:

Trust God from the bottom of your heart; don't try to figure out everything on your own. Listen for God's voice in everything you do, everywhere you go; he's the one who will keep you on the right track. Don't assume that you know it all. Run to God! Run from evil; Your body will glow with health; your very bones will vibrate with life! Honor God with everything you own; give him the first and the best. Your barns will burst, your wine vats will brim over, but don't, my son, resent God's discipline; don't sulk under his loving correction. It's the child he loves that God corrects; a father's delight is behind all this.

Is it possible for adults to, *"Trust God from the bottom of your heart; don't try to figure out everything on your own. Listen for God's voice in everything you do, everywhere you go; he's the one who will keep you on the right track"*? Think of it this way. Jesus is in your living room and looks you in the eye, calls you by name, and says, "Daughter, trust me from the bottom of your heart. Don't try to figure anything out on your own. Let me help you. Listen for me and our Father in everything you do. He will keep you on the right track. We are in this together, no matter what." Through tears, I pen this portion. Jesus wants to sit with me and help me, to assure me that his love for me is great and that I can trust him from the bottom of my heart. I want my boys to trust me from the bottom of their hearts. Our heavenly Father wants us to do the same. As a child, we are able to trust from the bottom of our hearts; it is just in our nature.

This is where your life can change. Cry out to God and ask him to help you do this. Don't put the responsibility on yourself. Take one small step today to trust God. To see him as your Father and begin to trust him from the bottom of your heart.

"Don't assume that you know it all." Jesus continues by making it clear to us that we don't know much. We need his help. This isn't a dig at us or to make us feel bad. It is actually a relief for us. He is saying, "This world is far more complex than human thought. You are in a spiritual war. But I have overcome the world. Let me help you and guide you. You don't need to press through; you need to trust me. I am the Creator. *'I am the way, the truth, and the life'* (John 14:6). You don't need to know; I know. Your stress will disappear when you stop making all of your own decisions. I won't push myself on you; you have a free will. But if you ask me to help you, *'I am standing at the door.'* Run to me and let me be your shield. I find my joy in protecting you."

"Run to God! Run from evil." When we are little, we practically run everywhere we go. We have tremendous energy. If we want to swing, we run to the swing. If we want an ice cream cone, we run to get ice cream. If we want to jump in the water, we run to the pool. We run, and we run some more. Jesus is saying, "Run to your Father, and run away from evil. Run and don't look back. Run in the right direction. Run as fast as you can into the arms of the Father. Run to life. God is waiting with his arms open. He will sweep you off your feet, hug you, and whisk you up to his shoulders. Run!"

"Your body will glow with health, your very bones will vibrate with life! Honor God with everything you own; give him the first and the best. Your barns will burst, your wine vats will brim over." When we trust Jesus, our bodies glow in health. This makes perfect sense. When we trust Jesus, our bodies no longer go through the stress of responsibility. Stress brings heart problems, strain, fatigue, headaches, stomach issues, and so on. Stress brings dis-ease, better known as disease. Jesus is telling us that when we trust him from the bottom of our hearts, our hearts will be healthy, and we will glow with health. Glowing with health means you are healthy in all directions; healthy from the inside out. You have removed the stress and replaced it with food (God's Word) that will satisfy your entire life.

God also promises to prosper you. Basically, you will never need anything. As you give him your first and best, you are making an eternal trade signified by God's own promise. He promises to give you more than you will need as you give him your very best. You love him with your very best, and he gives you what you need, God's very best.

"But don't, my son, resent God's discipline; don't sulk under his loving correction. It's the child he loves that God corrects; a father's delight is behind all this." In the end, it is up to us to seek God and respect his discipline. As children, we need to understand that his delight is behind all of his corrections. It is essential to begin to make changes as we walk in the love of the Lord.

Jesus warns us about not throwing temper tantrums when things don't go our way. It is easy to sulk. Most children are masters at the manipulation of sulking. My puppy, Pendleton, is very good at sulking. The phrase, puppy dog eyes, is perfected when Pendleton is corrected. We sulk when we don't get our way. We sulk when we think we are overlooked. We sulk because our favorite coffee creamer is sold out. Humans are expert sulkers. Jesus is asking us to step up and understand all corrections are for our benefit. As we learn, we can be trusted more, and we trust God more.

We need to understand Jesus is real. We need to trust like children do. We need the hope and joy of our inner child. We need to be lifted on our Daddy's shoulders and feel the strength of his body to safely get us home. Nothing can replace the solidarity of the footsteps of our Father taking us home. Come, daughter, and grow up by becoming a child once again. Take his hand.

Try It

1. Use the Scripture in Proverbs to create reminders all over your house in regard to trusting the Lord from the bottom of your heart.
2. Spend time with your Father, getting to know how much he loves you.
3. Read Ephesians 3:17–19 and meditate on the empowerment of understanding the love of God.
4. Decree with your own tongue that you are a child of God, loved perfectly.

Scripture: These words I speak to you are not incidental additions to your life, homeowner improvements to your standard of living. They are foundational words, words to build a life on. If you work these words into your life, you are like a smart carpenter who built his house on solid rock. Rain poured down, the river flooded, a tornado hit- but nothing moved that house. It was fixed to the rock. But if you just use my words in Bible studies and don't work them into your life, you are like a stupid carpenter who built his house on the sandy beach. When a storm rolled in and the waves came up, it collapsed like a house of cards. Matthew 7:24-27

3

"If you train hard, you'll not only be hard, you'll be hard to beat." —Herschel Walker[6]

The Right Stuff

Does the Equipment Matter?

Focus: I am smeared with the Word of God, anointed for battle.

Scripture: Finally, be strong in the Lord and his mighty power. Put on the full armor of God, so that you can take your stand against the devil's schemes. Ephesians 6:10

It is the end of the day, and I come home from work. I am tired! My mind is drained, and my body is exhausted. I want to take a nap. However, it is gym time. I don't really want to go. My mind comes up with plenty of excuses. "I can go tomorrow." "I am not too out of shape." "I look good for my age." Yep, the mind runs wild. I need a change of perspective. I hear my trainer's words, "Don't be upset with the results you didn't get with the work you didn't do." I pray for a new attitude. How can I prepare myself to go to the gym? It is as easy as changing my clothes. It is time to become an athlete.

I look at myself in the mirror, "Come on, athlete, let's go do this." Ask any athlete, does the equipment matter? You better believe it matters. "Americans alone spend 90.9 billion dollars a year on sports equipment," Sarah O Brian.[7] As a group, we are fine with spending our hard-earned money on the right clothes, shoes, gloves, headphones, and other gear just to go workout or play. Yes, the equipment matters.

Changing into my clothes:

- I love Athleta! Athleta is stretchy, pliable, returns to its natural shape, and holds things in place. Yep, it is better!
- Shoes: Are CrossFit shoes a necessity? I didn't think so until I wore them. I realize that for the stability and balance I need, they are better. These shoes keep me from rocking around. In a world full of weights, balance is essential.
- Gloves: I hate blisters! Twisting in my hands plus heavy weights equals blisters. I wear protection. Gloves help me lift, work hard, and do what I need to do.
- Contacts: I want to be able to see clearly without my glasses banging up and down on my nose.
- Hair: It is pulled up and out of my face.
- Headphones: I need music to help keep me focused and at the right tempo.

Standing in the bedroom, I look and feel like an athlete, ready for battle. I am prepared mentally and physically. It is time to strengthen the mind, body, and spirit. It is time to hit it! I wonder, *Do I prepare myself daily for the workout of life?* Just like consistent time in the gym builds muscle, spending time with God builds spiritual muscle. If I go through this preparation daily just to strengthen my body, why will I not fight with the same tenacity for my walk with the Lord? Satan knows the Bible and knows me. He is here to steal, kill, and destroy my life. I realize that if I am not prepared to fight him, he will take me out, out the door . . .

The cool thing is that God knows the equipment we need to be successful in life. He sent Jesus, and Jesus left us protected. In Ephesians 6:10–18, it says:

Finally, be strong in the Lord and his mighty power. Put on the full armor of God, so that you can take your stand against the devil's schemes. For we are not fighting against people made of flesh and blood, but against the evil rulers and authorities of an unseen world, against those mighty powers of darkness who rule this world, and against wicked spirits in the heavenly realms. Use every piece of God's armor to resist the enemy in time of evil, so that after the battle you will still be standing firm. Stand your ground, putting on the sturdy belt of truth and the body armor of God's righteousness. For shoes, put on peace that comes from the Good News, so that you will be fully prepared. In every battle you will need faith as your shield to stop the fiery arrows aimed at you by Satan. Put on salvation as your helmet, and take the sword of the Spirit, which is the word of God. Pray at all times and on every occasion in the power of the Holy Spirit. Stay alert and be persistent in your prayers for all Christians everywhere.

Let's look at each one of these verses in more depth.

"Finally, be strong in the Lord and his mighty power." Be strong in whom? Be strong in the Lord and his mighty power. It isn't up to you. It is up to the one who made you. God is the creator. It is our job to feast on the strength of our Creator. God created Lucifer, and Lucifer created his own pride and defeat. God isn't concerned with Lucifer, the accuser. He is a defeated foe. Yet, the accuser will tell God's children that we are defeated. He will spit fire and lie to us to hurt the Lord. This Scripture should give us hope in the understanding that God's mighty power is available to us and that our strength comes from him.

"Put on the full armor of God, so that you can take your stand against the devil's schemes." Take your stand! Take your stand! Stand up and look the devil in the eye and let him know you will take a stand for those you love, the salvation of the lost, the job you want, the health of your family, the peace that belongs to you, and the finances you need for the kingdom. Become the child God intends you to be. Do not bow at the accuser's feet. Do not allow him the upper hand. Dig deep within the Word of God and stand upon the promises the Lord has given us. Be bold and take a stand.

Satan is a schemer, one who has a systematic plan or arrangement for attaining some object or putting some idea into effect. He wants you to believe the circumstance you see rather than the truth of God's Word. He wants to focus your reality on the world; he wants you to believe the reality of your circumstances, not the Word of God. He makes plans in a devious way or with intent to create an illusion in your life. You must take the reality of Scripture and exchange it for the reality of your circumstances. *"Call those things which are not as though they were"* (Romans. 4:17).

"Use every piece of God's armor to resist the enemy in time of evil, so that after the battle you will still be standing firm." Each piece is as important as the other; leave nothing out. Use everything the Lord gives you in battle. Do not try to fight without his protection and strength. Resistance is difficult, and the accuser is a contender for your soul. He is standing in the other corner looking at you, deciding on his game plan. He has been watching your entire life and knows the sequence of punches to throw at you. He isn't stupid and has a team in place to strike and strike hard. He will have combinations in place and strategies for harm that thrive on weaknesses. Put on each piece and think specifically about the importance of each one. Be fully dressed, daily! He will continue to be in the opposite corner, but you will be standing firm.

"Stand your ground, putting on the sturdy belt of truth and the body armor of God's righteousness." In America, there is a law called the stand-your-ground law (sometimes called the "line in the sand" or "no duty to retreat" law). This law establishes a right by which a person may defend oneself or others (right of self-defense) against threats or perceived threats, even to the point of applying lethal force. The Lord is telling us to stand our ground against the schemer. To a Christian, our lethal force is the truth of God's Word and armor of his righteousness. God's Word trumps any opposition of the accuser. If we can muster the strength to decree God's Word into a situation without allowing fear to create doubt, then we will see victory. We must get that first win, so that we can begin a new pattern of thought. We will begin to trust God in every situation because we have seen the victory. Trusting God can be very difficult, but it is the only way to live life.

Let's look back at the time when Jesus was drawing in the sand. In John 8, Jesus has returned to the Mount of Olives, and the Pharisees brought a woman they had caught in the act of adultery. In verse 4, the Pharisees asked, *"'Teacher,' they said to Jesus, 'this woman was caught in the very act of adultery. The law of Moses says to stone her. What do you say?'"* Verse 6: *"They were trying to trap him into saying something they could use against him, but Jesus stooped down and wrote in the dust with his finger."* Do not let the devil trap you into saying something that goes against the truth of God's Word. This is an easy trap to find ourselves in. When we see the outcome of a situation as bleak or scary, it is very easy to say what we see. At that point, our words are at war with the truth of God's Word, which leads to our own demise. When God says to put on the armor of truth, he wants us to speak his truth to a situation that may not be positive. Don't let the reality that stands in front of you transform the reality of what you expect to be the result. We must learn to speak the truth to any and all situations of life.

Jesus's final response is found in verses 7 and 10: *"All right, stone her. But let those who have never sinned throw the first stone!"* Jesus defended the woman from the perceived threat of the Pharisees. The truth relieved the woman of a lethal threat. He gave himself some time to hear his Father's voice before he spoke. He spoke the truth of God's Word into the situation, which ultimately changed the outcome. *"The woman was then asked by Jesus, 'Where are your accusers? Didn't even one of them condemn you?' 'No, Lord,' she said. And Jesus said, 'Neither do I. Go and sin no more.'"* When Jesus spoke God's Word into the situation, the woman was not condemned. Similar to this woman, we are not condemned in the situations of life. When we speak God's Word, no matter the circumstance, we are not condemned, and the Lord can move on our behalf and change the outcome. Yes, speaking the truth of God's Word must be our strategy in battle.

"For shoes, put on peace that comes from the Good News, so that you will be fully prepared." Peace should be on your feet. One of the definitions of a shoe(s)[3] is: a device that retards, stops, or controls the motion of an object. Looking at the last part of this definition, we find that a shoe controls the motion of an object. As Christians, what do we want to control the motion of our life? Shouldn't we want to move in the peace of the Lord? Whether we are striving for a new financial opportunity or need to handle a human situation, we should be walking in peace. Jesus said in John 14:27, *"Peace I leave with you; my peace. I give you. I do not give to you as the world gives. Do not let your hearts be troubled and do not be afraid."* The message version adds a little more depth, *"I am leaving you well and whole. That's my parting gift to you. Peace. I don't leave you the way you're used to being left—feeling abandoned, bereft. So don't be upset. Don't be distraught."* We don't go around looking for peace. We may temporarily give it up or not use it, but we don't have to go find it. Peace is ours, always!

Shoes also provide grip and protection from wear or damage. How do we withstand the onset of attacks without peace? How do we wear out the devil without peace? How can we pray for others without peace? What was the one thing that didn't wear out on the Israelites after forty years? God gave their shoes supernatural strength to not break, crack, or fall apart after forty years of walking. If we want balance, stability, protection,

---

[3] Webster's 1828 American Dictionary of the English Language, Walking Lion Press, West Valley City, UT, 2010.

strength, and support, then we must put on our shoes of peace. Lace them up tight and move as we hear the voice of the Lord, remembering to only take the steps in the direction of peace.

"In every battle you will need faith as your shield to stop the fiery arrows aimed at you by Satan." When we look at this verse, what picture is formed in your mind? Consider an arrow aimed at you with precision and speed, an arrow full of fire, ready to cause damage to you and those you love, not a single arrow, but multiple arrows sent at once to inflict pain. A shield is a defensive armor piece. It is for protection. How can our faith become our protection? How can faith be a shield? What if our faith isn't very strong?

What if we look at faith in its purest sense: belief and trust in; loyalty to God. We trust God without question. We believe in his goodness no matter what. Even if our prayers are unanswered, can we trust God without question? Think about a shield being your main protection, whether it is tied to your chest or on your arm; it is the one thing that stops Satan's arrows. Can we trust God to protect us in all situations no matter what? Our duty is to rise up the shield with complete trust that God will defend and protect us. It is our trust in God that allows his Word to protect us. We must have the faith to use our shields.

"Put on salvation as your helmet, and take the sword of the Spirit, which is the word of God." The job of a helmet is to protect the head. Motorcyclists are encouraged to wear helmets as preservation of the brain in case of an accident. God considers salvation as our helmet. We are to place his salvation around the mind. We are to remember his forgiveness as our deliverance from anything that comes against us. As the mind wonders, reasons, and worries, the Lord reminds us to cover the battleground in his forgiveness. The mind can become a

playground to Satan if we do not surround it in the salvation of the Lord. Coupled with the helmet is the sword of the Spirit, which is the Word of God. Unlike the shield, the sword is offensive. A sword*(s)* is a weapon with a long blade for cutting or thrusting that is often used as a symbol of honor or authority.[4]How about that! God gave us a sword because we are honored and have authority. Our big brother Jesus took all the pain, suffering, and the wrath of God when he went to the cross. In return, we became forgiven and honored. Jesus sits at the right hand of God. When the accuser comes, Jesus looks at his Father and defends us because we belong to him. Jesus speaks on our behalf. The word Jesus speaks cuts the accusations of the devil. God only hears the words of Jesus on our behalf. This is what truly occurs in the courts of heaven, but on earth, we can allow the accuser a right into our lives if we do not line our tongues up with the Word of God.

Consider for a moment the words from your mouth act like a sword, then think of how they bring life or death into a situation. Proverbs 18:21 says, *"The tongue has the power of life and death, and those who love it will eat its fruit."* The Message version says, *"Words kill, words give life; they're either poison or fruit- you choose."* Poison or fruit, you choose. You choose. I choose every time I say something to speak life or death into that situation. Maybe we should all spend more time drawing in the sand and waiting for God to give us words. Maybe I should begin to see words as a sword that is meant for aggression. It is time to see words as an offensive tool used to bring life to the dead. Romans 4:17: *"The God who gives life to the dead and calls*

---

[4] Webster's 1828 American Dictionary of the English Language, Walking Lion Press, West Valley City, UT, 2010.

things that are not as though they were." It is time to give the Word of God first place in life.

"Pray at all times and on every occasion in the power of the Holy Spirit. Stay alert and be persistent in your prayers for all Christians everywhere." Prayer is the main example Jesus set before us. He went off by himself and prayed. He stopped and listened to the Father. He honored God before he performed miracles. Jesus knew something we didn't about the power of prayer. Looking at this Scripture, it says to pray at all times and on every occasion. How often is prayer a last resort, sidebar, or an afterthought? However, this Scripture says to pray at all times. Always pray. Always pray. This means God wants to be included in the smallest detail in our lives. He wants the privilege to direct our lives. We must ask him to do so. We must pray and invite God into every situation. Consider prayer as a deliberate form of communication with God. Prayer is our way of talking with God. Just begin to invite the Lord into your daily life. Spend time with him and ask him for directions. Use your normal voice and just speak with him like a friend.

To understand the fullness and importance of prayer, read John 17. In this chapter, Jesus prayed for himself, his disciples, and his future followers. He left no one out. He prays for all of us. He took the time to pray for us. He had a connection with our Father and knew how essential prayer was. Jesus was our example of how to live. If he spent a large portion of his life in prayer, then we should too. Jesus wanted us to know the Father as he did. He wanted to glorify the Father and wanted us to be able to talk with God. He wanted us to see the goodness of his Father. As Jesus returned to the Father and left us here, he gave us the example of prayer so that we would never be alone. He wanted us to understand that we have a line to heaven. We have a line to our Creator. We are heard in the heavenly places. We are loved. Jesus says in John 17:15, *"I'm not asking that you take them out of this world, but that you guard them from the Evil one."* Jesus cared enough about all of us to ask God to protect us from the evil one. He left us protected and gave us his peace.

God has always placed importance on the way we dress. In Exodus 28:4, God changed the clothes of the men who were to lead the Israelites after they had left Egypt and were to move into the promised land. God had rescued his people from the oppression of the Egyptians. He told them they needed a change of clothes. You see, they needed new clothes to begin new thoughts. God wanted them clothed and anointed in him so they could serve those in their charge. Exodus 28:2:

> *Make special clothing for Aaron to show his separation to God-beautiful garments that will lend dignity to his work. Instruct all those who have special skills as tailors to make the garments that will set Aaron apart from everyone else, so he may serve me as a priest. They are to make a chest piece, an ephod, a robe, an embroidered tunic, a turban, and a sash. They will also make special garments for Aaron's sons to wear when they serve as priests before me.*

These clothes were made of fine linen cloth with gold, blue, purple, and scarlet yarn, which represents royalty. God was detailed in the manner in which He dressed them. We are royalty and belong to him. He wants us to be the victor in all we do.

God wants man to carry out his will on earth. We must be willing to prepare ourselves for this mission. We must be fully clothed in the armor of God, praying at all times, and understanding the words that flow from our mouths to change situations.

Getting dressed:

- Stand your ground
- Go through
- Stand again
- Be prepared
- Pray at all times
- Stay alert
- Be persistent

This is how we fight our battles and develop our inner champion.

Try It:

1. Go for a walk daily if possible.
2. Find alone time with God each day.

Scripture: *"I am smeared with the word of God, anointed for battle"* (Eph. 6:10).

4

"The world ain't all sunshine and rainbows. It's a very mean and nasty place, and I don't care how tough you are, it will beat you to your knees and keep you there permanently if you let it. You, me, nobody is gonna hit as hard as life."

—*Sylvester Stallone as Rocky Balboa*[8]

True Fight

How Much Grit Do You Have?

Focus: For every sin, there is a sacrifice.

Scripture: Jesus went out as usual to the Mount of Olives, and his disciples followed him. On reaching the place, he said to them, "Pray that you will not fall into temptation." He withdrew about a stone's throw beyond them, knelt down and prayed, "Father, if you are willing take this cup from me; yet not my will, but yours be done." An angel from heaven appeared to him and strengthened him. And being in anguish, he prayed more earnestly, and his sweat was like drops of blood falling to the ground (Luke 22:39–44).

It is dark. The air is sour with lingering, rancid smells of blood. Wailing and moaning surrounds this moment in time; death is coming. Punches are flying through the air, accompanied by sweat running from the pores. It is dirty, ugly, and painful. The body begs for rest as the tense arms and legs become exhaustively heavy. Rest will not come; it is only the beginning. The louder the cries belt out, the harder the hits come. Great drops of blood spew from the eyes and the temple. The cries get louder, and the crowd is rotten. Lash after lash, it won't stop.

Spit, profane words, jeers, and taunts are on the lips of all who watch the brutal fight. Time seems to fade; pain does not. You want to say anything just to make the torment stop. You scream at the top of your lungs, no answer. Sacrifice is the only word in the mind. No one is in your corner, not even God. *What a phony*, stirs in your subconscious. *No one believes in this God of yours.* Someone stands to accuse. Someone is laughing at you. Not only that, but someone hates you. *Go ahead, pray, you won't get an answer. How stupid can you be? Where is this God of yours? Everyone will face the end of life.*

Yes, death is loud, cruel, and persistent. He stands on the opposite side of the ring. I am targeted for permanent destruction. He hates me with utter defiance and absolute repugnance. In the middle of this whirlwind, who is in the fight? Is it me? Is it Jesus? It is both. Jesus was the sacrifice; he was the ultimate lamb. Satan hates him, and he hates us because of him.

It seems, at times, the louder we call out, the more silent things become. The stronger we pray, the more that comes against us. Sometimes the only thought is trust, the only word—Jesus. Even mighty men of God, great prayer warriors, battled the devil. One particular story in the Old Testament relates to a prayer from Daniel. Daniel sent up a prayer that was heard by

God. God sent an angel to handle Daniel's request. The angel was held up by Satan for twenty-one days. Therefore, the Lord sent Michael, the archangel of battle, to work on Daniel's behalf. *"But the prince of the Persian kingdom resisted me twenty-one days. Then Michael, one of the chief princes, came to help me, because I was detained there with the king of Persia"* (Dan. 10:13). The king of Persia is in reference to Satan. Make no mistake, you have an enemy, and his name is Lucifer, Satan, or the accuser. He hates us with a passion unlike any other. *"He comes to kill, steal, and destroy"* (John 10:10).

Satan uses death. God creates life. Deception is Satan's strongest force. He hides in it. He uses fog and perception to confuse and scare people. He works to create illusions in your life that become real in your mind. Satan hates life. He would rather eliminate it than allow people the choice to love God. Abortion is one of his biggest falsities. He brainwashes women to the thought that it is a choice to reject life. He suggests a baby would be too big of a burden or would bring shame to a family. The fog of fear is used to scare women into a choice of death. This choice can never be reversed, and it will haunt the decision maker long after the baby is gone.

Making God suffer is Satan's mission. He wants God to be in anguish over every sin man makes. Millions of tears are drenched on every spirit that wasn't allowed to live. Jesus has sweet words for those who make such terrible mistakes, *"Forgive them Father, for they know not what they do,"* Luke 23:34. Satan uses God's own creation against him to break his heart. Where love isn't present, there is only death.

In Matthew 5:8, the Word says, *"Blessings come when your eyes are pure. Blindness comes when your eyes are cloudy."* Bringing glory to the Lord's goodness is what Satan works the hardest to remove. In the movie, *Jurassic Park*,[9] the characters need to reset the protection devices. In order to do so, they need to get to a compound that is away from the main building. As two of the characters begin their trek to the new building, they are warned about the velociraptors hiding in the jungle. The warning comes in reference to how the dinosaurs hunt. Be careful of the raptor to the side. He is the one who targets the prey. The one facing you is just a decoy. In life, Satan will use surprise attacks to derail your faith. He often comes in from the side.

Spending time with God is the only way to recognize and fight the attacks. Time with him allows the fullness of his love to attach to us. You must be attached to him to be victorious. Some battles are so intense; you must trust the Word and the name—Jesus.

Know your enemy.

Eve was a child of God. She was Adam's best friend. She was given control of the planet. Furthermore, she was allowed to walk in the garden God had created. She was given complete freedom to roam as she liked. She was a precious child to the Lord, and she was adored. Satan hated her.

Satan is clever and crafty. Beginning in Genesis 3:1, he questioned Eve, *"Do I understand that God told you not to eat from (any) tree in the garden?"* Why does he do this? He uses trickery and partial truth to get me or you to reason rather than trust in God. His purpose is to use part of the truth to create wandering thoughts (doubts) to make us weigh sides. He comes at our confidence we have in God in subtle glimmers of opposite thoughts.

Most of the time, our initial response, if we know God, is strong. We feel safe and steadfast in our answers. *"Not at all,"*

Eve answered in a strong and determined voice. *"We can eat from the trees in the garden,"* Genesis 3:2. This is where Eve should have stopped. She should have been done with the accuser. Satan doesn't deserve the time it takes for conversation. Why waste time debating with someone who wants you dead?

As she continued, she gave Satan a doorway. *"It is only about the tree in the middle of the garden that God said, 'don't eat from it, don't even touch it, or you'll die,"* Genesis 3:3. What did God mean by "you'll die"? He meant your peace will die. Your shelter in him will die. You will see the ugly side of life. All will change and sadness will be shown. God wasn't worried about his own authority; he was concerned for her purity. *"You won't die,"* the accuser answered, Genesis 3:4. Die is exactly what he wanted her to do.

The enemy answered her with the truth. *"You won't die."* Physically, she would not die; spiritually, she would. Satan was after her purity, innocence, and joy. Satan was after her spirit. He was ready to drop her to her knees by removing God's protection. He stole her keys. He continued, *"God knows that the moment you eat from that tree, you'll see what is really going on. You'll be just like God, knowing everything, ranging all the way from good to evil,"* Genesis 3:5. He was right. He spoke the truth. He is good at that. He told her exactly what would happen. What she didn't know, because she was so loved, was the ugly side of evil.

She didn't know what life looked like outside of God, which is all Satan had left, life without God. I think that is why God allowed Satan to continue to live. God thought, *okay you want to live without me? Go ahead.* I don't think Lucifer had any idea what living without the love of God would be like until it happened. Once it did, he was certain these humans would understand his pain. He would take pleasure in their destruction.

Who is Satan exactly, and why does he hate God so much? Satan was an angel. His name was Lucifer. He was the archangel of praise. He was majestic, beautiful, and full of sound. His body was dazzled by instruments of all types. Glowing instruments encompassed his being. He was loved, and he had a place.

In Ezekiel 28:6, we get a very close look at the angel Lucifer. Ezekiel, a prophet of God, was ascribing as the Lord began to tell him about an earthly king. Through this king, we will begin to understand who Lucifer is.

Beginning in verse 6: *"Because you think you are wise, wise as a god, I am going to bring foreigners against you."* Verse 8 continues, *"They will bring you down to the pit, and you will die a violent death."* This king had been identified as having the characteristics of Lucifer. Lucifer was confident in who he was. He considered himself to be equal with God. The Lord spoke of this king as if he was Lucifer. The following verses are more of a description of who Lucifer was when he was in heaven, even to the detail of the king being thrown into a pit, which is Satan's eternal home.

It is important to understand who Lucifer was, how he fell to become Satan, and how he remains the accuser today. Lucifer was an archangel, one of three most adored creatures. Ezekiel 28:11: *"You were a seal of perfection, full of wisdom, and perfect beauty. You were in Eden, the garden of God' every precious stone adorned you: carnelian, chrysolite, emerald, topaz, onyx, jasper, lapis lazuli, turquoise, and beryl."* These gems are found in the foundational stones of God's kingdom. They are found in Revelation 3. I have studied the colors at length, and the Lord has shown me the importance of the color and the stone. All of the precious gems have meaning. When each stone was hand placed in Lucifer, it represented a characteristic of God. For example, the onyx stone represents protection. It is a jet-black stone with God's power to protect and provide security. Beryl, on the other hand, is a light blue stone similar to aquamarine. Beryl represents youth, truth, and clarity. It holds happiness and blessing.

God placed amazing power and understanding inside of Lucifer. He hand selected each gem and carefully placed it inside the angel. Therefore, the accuser has many weapons at his disposal. He understands so many aspects of our lives because he was given the understanding by God. Why is this essential for the believer to understand? As believers, we need to know who we battle against. Picture, in heaven, God creating Lucifer, adorned in jewels, each with its own significance, carefully placed at the perfect location. He became full of who God is. We need to realize that the accuser will use any means possible to place fear in our hearts. Fear makes us react in ways we would not normally choose.

Continuing in Ezekiel 28:13: *"Your settings and mountings were made of gold; on the day you were created they were prepared. Beauty and strength bonded together to hold everything in place. You were anointed as a guardian cherub, for I so ordained you."* Lucifer was ordained by God. He was placed as a guardian to protect and love the Lord. He was of great beauty and held together by pure gold. He was precious to the Lord. In other words, God spared nothing when he created Lucifer. He was beautiful, creative, intelligent, strong, and full of wisdom. He was a winged angelic being who attended to God. He was an angel in the highest courts.

Ezekiel 28:15: *"You were blameless in your ways from the days you were created."* Yes, Lucifer was blameless. He had no responsibility for a fault or wrong. He had no guilt or liability. Consider this for a moment. The blameless cherub is now the demon accuser. What God created him not to be is exactly who he is. Lucifer, who was to find no fault with anyone, now stands before God and Jesus to accuse and blame every man, woman, and child. This is a significant understanding. If we, as children of God, can find our rightful standing through Jesus, then the accuser can only accuse. He cannot win. If we can understand that his only job now is to blame and lie for the purpose of condemnation, then he cannot begin to defeat us. We must understand that the only way to defeat Lucifer is to plead the blood of Jesus on our lives daily. How did this supreme angel become so twisted?

Lucifer had a problem—servanthood.

Lucifer wanted to be God. He did not want to serve him. He did not want to be under the Lord. He wanted his own way, ideas, kingdom, and servants. He was not going to perform acts of service to God. I wish I understood what the conversation must have been like between God and Lucifer when Lucifer challenged him. All of that remains a mystery to me. But the one thing I do understand is that these Scriptures are in the Bible for a purpose, not for the purpose of frightening us but to make us aware of just how much we need Jesus. We are humans, and God and Satan are spirits. We do not war against flesh and blood. We war against spirits. God wanted us to see that without his protection through the blood of Christ, we are naked, frail, and alone. We cannot begin to fight battles with the accuser without the Word, the armor, and the blood.

Know your enemy.

When God created earth for man, he created all the creatures as well. The archangel Lucifer was reduced to the form of a snake. His name was changed from Lucifer to Satan or the accuser. Therefore, he, like all the other creatures, were placed under man's control. Lucifer, an angel of the Most High, was now demoted to be under the command of Adam. God favored man even above angels because he was created in God's image. The keys of the earth were handed to man, and with those keys, all authority. Can you imagine the hatred Satan had for man? He went from angel to snake. Lucifer, a servant in God's inner courts, was now under the control of man. He was angry. He wasn't going to allow it. How could he now serve a human? He despised serving God. No way. So, his new mission: take out humans. His mission today: TAKE OUT HUMANS!

As I sit in my kitchen today writing this book, death is being loosened on earth at a rapid pace. Abortion, suicide, YouTube videos, cyber bullying, and broken families are at a record high. It has been interesting, as I pen these words, to recognize how Satan seems to have upped his game of destruction. Maybe it is because I am spending so much time with God right now and am able to see what is truly happening in the spirit, or maybe God is giving me a deeper understanding, but I realize now how committed Satan is to our destruction. He wants us dead. For those of us who have given our lives to Jesus, he can't ever get our spirits back. He knows we belong to God, and there is nothing he can do about that.

So, if we are eternally heaven bound, what can he possibly do to harm us? He goes after anyone we love. He purposefully creates situations of torment to make our lives on earth as miserable as possible. He kills people and relationships all around us to get us to question God's love. He wants us to view God as harsh, mean, or unforgiving. He doesn't want us to see him as our Father. I am learning Satan's goal. He truly wants to eliminate life before it ever gets the opportunity to love God. For example, teenage suicide is a means of ripping a young life out of the hands of God. Loud, screaming thoughts of hatred and loneliness bring limited options into the minds of young people who do not know how to cope with the enemy. He tricks them into thinking there is no way out. Satan went after Eve with a vengeance. He comes after us with the same animosity.

As we return to Eve, we need to understand that while he spoke, he had an ulterior motive. Satan jeered, "Eat, eat, eat so I can steal everything God so carefully created for you. You spoiled, created-in-God's-image human. I hate you. Eat, and I'll snatch the keys to earth right out of your hands. I loathe you!" Genesis 3:6: *"When the Woman saw that the tree looked like good eating and realized what she should get out of it—she would know everything! —she took and ate the fruit and then gave some to her husband, and he ate. Immediately, the two of them did 'see what's really going on'—saw themselves naked!"* Verse 8 continues, *"When they heard the sound of God strolling through the garden in the evening breeze, the Man and his Wife hid in the trees of the garden, hid from God."*

This is the saddest story in the Bible. They hid from God. Let that sink in for a moment. How many times have we hidden from God? How many times have we felt anxious before him? How many times have we made the wrong choice? Adam and Eve were created for the pleasure of God. He gave them everything. He wanted to be their father. He walked with them in the garden. He loved them. Satan stole every bit of that security right out from underneath them. He stole their innocence, and through their choice, we became naked too. God's heart was broken, and Satan laughed.

God had a plan, and his name was Jesus.

Jesus went out as usual to the Mount of Olives, and his disciples followed him. On reaching the place, he said to them, "Pray that you will not fall into temptation." He withdrew about a stone's throw beyond them, and prayed, "Father, if you are willing take this cup from me; yet not my will, but yours be done." An angel from heaven appeared to him and strengthened him. And being in anguish, he prayed more earnestly, and his sweat was like drops of blood falling to the ground (Luke 22:39–44).

Try It:

1. Read the entire story of Adam and Eve in Genesis 3.
2. Go for a walk and invite Jesus to join you.
3. Ask the Lord to give you peace from your mistakes.
4. Listen to Christian music.

5

"When we are children we seldom think of the future. This innocence leaves us free to enjoy ourselves as few adults can. The day we fret about the future is the day we leave our childhood behind." —Patrick Rothfuss[10]

Rocks and Giggles

Who Will Help You Grow?

Focus: Take him by the hand.

Scripture: He called a little child to him and placed the child among them. And he said: "Truly I tell you, unless you change and become like little children, you will never enter the kingdom of heaven. Therefore, whoever takes the lowly position of this child is the greatest in the kingdom of heaven. And whoever welcomes one such child in my name welcomes me" (Matt. 18:1–5).

In a tiny little town in Texas, a tiny little girl is growing up. She has brownish blond hair that is straight as a board. She is brown from the sun kissing her, and she is very happy. Outside is the place she likes to be. With the soft wind and gentle warmth, she spends most of her days talking with someone quite special. She is happy. She walks around looking for rocks and the occasional puddle left by the rain. She listens as he talks with her. She likes to listen because this man truly understands her. It's like he made her. She isn't sure how he knows so much, but one thing is for sure, she adores him. As they walk, he talks with her about how trees are made and how rivers of life are everywhere. He shows her the mountains and gives her hope for the future. In her mind, there is no one quite like her best friend. As they continue to walk, he tells her that as she grows up, there is nothing she can't do. He tells her how much he loves her and that he will always be with her. This young girl has no reason to doubt. She just giggles. She is happy.

As they continue to walk, she takes him by the hand. She feels a peace that passes all understanding. She asks him, "Jesus, do you love everyone the same way you love me? Do you spend time like this with my friends?" In the middle of this conversation, she can't imagine that he spends time like this with anyone else, but deep in her heart, she hopes he does. Jesus gently smiles and says, "Of course, I do. You are all very special to me." They talk back and forth, and she wonders why he loves her so much. But down deep in her spirit, she knows this love is real. This love is never-ending; this love is eternal. There is nothing like this afternoon in Texas, this afternoon with Jesus.

It is many years down the road, and this same girl still goes outside to play with Jesus. She is older now, almost fifty, but somehow when she walks outside into the gentle warm sun, she feels like she is five again. There is nothing like taking Jesus by the hand and feeling like a child. Now, she and Jesus have been through life. The promises of yesterday have been walked through. One thing remains, he has never left her side. She is married now and has a beautiful family. She is professional and has success. She has a beautiful home and great friends. She is married to an amazing man. Somehow, as she remembers those quiet days as she grew up, she realizes that her friend Jesus was right. He has always been beside her, and he is the one who created her.

Now, their talks mostly revolve around her kids and her life choices. Her questions ruminate on what he needs her to do. She asks him about her purpose and next steps. However, through all of those discussions, he somehow leads her back to how much he loves her. He reminds her to follow her heart and not worry so much about the future. He has placed his Word in her heart, and he nudges her to speak it out. Although their talks are more "grown up," he wants her to continue to trust him with childlike faith. She is happy.

On certain days, she takes him by the hand and cries. Things haven't gone the way she planned. She is confused and doesn't understand. Her mind wants to reason, and she needs answers. One of her dear friends has a child with leukemia, and there are no answers. Suffering is running wild, and the enemy has targeted a baby. In her heart, she knows this isn't God's plan, but she wonders how to fight him. She has learned of Scripture and knows of her authority, but when things are not changing, then what? She goes outside and talks with Jesus. He takes her by the hand and loves her. He whispers hope and help. He tells her there are battles that are very difficult to fight. There are times when she does not see the unseen. Fortunately, Jesus is able to take care of the problems she cannot. He reminds her that he took care of this baby over 2000 years ago. Isaiah 53:5: *"He was wounded for our transgressions; he was bruised for our iniquities; the chastisement of our peace was upon him."*

He gives her strength in the fact that because this bothers her, this bothers him. He reminds her of the little girl she once was and the relationship he had with her. He asks, "Don't you realize I have the same relationship with this baby girl? I have not left her, and I won't leave her. My love for her is great, and I will not allow the enemy to steal her from me." There is quiet as her spirit settles. She knows, above anything else, Jesus can be trusted. Jeremiah 29:11 comes to her heart, *"'For I know the plans I have for you,' declares the LORD, 'plans to prosper you and not harm you, plans to give you hope and a future.'"*

"The LORD your God is with you, the Mighty Warrior who saves. He will take great delight in you; in his love he will no longer rebuke you but will rejoice over you with singing" (Zeph. 3:17). I love this verse because it is such an amazing combination of two things: war and singing. How is it possible to be at war and sing? Over the years, I have learned that to fight, you need to sing in the battle. You must give thanks in the valley. How do you fight when your hands are heavy, and your head is down? How can you gather strength if you cannot see a victory? Where can you possibly pull this kind of thankfulness when you are so tired? It comes from intimacy with Jesus before the war starts. Time with the Lord is the only way to fight the enemy.

The Lord, your God, is the mighty warrior who saves. He takes great delight in you and me. He is mighty regarding impressive power and strength. He is an experienced soldier, a warrior. His delight resounds through glory. God sees me under the protection of his Son, Jesus. My God, the experienced soldier whose power is intense, will demonstrate his glory on me and for me as I begin to praise and give thanks for all he has done.

When I was little, I spent most of my time with Jesus. Generations of prayer warriors lifted me up to the Lord before my feet ever touched the earth. I knew Jesus before I knew anyone. My mom prayed diligently for me, and I met Jesus for myself when I was around five. I gave my heart to him when I was eleven. I can honestly say I grew up with Jesus. He has always been central in my life. Many people cannot say that nor understand it. Many people have been lost for most of their lives. Some had no one praying for them. As I prepared to write this chapter, I asked myself over and over, "How can I show people this love? How can I possibly write a chapter that demonstrates this amazing person I know named Jesus?" Describing the King of kings is no easy task. I can only speak from experience. I can only hope the stories of my life can somehow connect to others in a way that they want to meet him.

Jesus came to earth for these reasons, YOU and me. He came to claim us as his own. He came to take us back from the enemy. There was only one way to accomplish this task: he had to die. Therefore, there is only one way to the Father, and that way is Jesus. No one else laid his life down to save people. No one else can bring us to God. Jesus is God's Son. Jesus laid down his life so we could return as sons and daughters. There is no other way. John 14:6: *"Jesus answered, 'I am the way and the truth and the life. No one comes to the Father except through me.'"* Jesus is the way.

Whether or not your childhood was innocent, or your current life is at peace, you can start today by making a simple choice; a choice to follow Christ. Jesus is willing to wait on you. *"Look at me. I stand at the door and knock. If you hear me call and*

open the door, I'll come right in and sit down to supper with you"
(Rev. 3:20). This is an invitation to intimacy, an invitation to a
new life. Jesus is asking to come into the door of your heart. He
wants to rearrange your furniture, or thoughts, to line up with
his Word. Once you begin to see things as he does, all things
become new; all things become possible.

Intimacy/s/ is a close familiarity or friendship with someone.[5] When you open the door to Jesus, you begin to build an
attachment to him. You begin to attach yourself to the Word of
God. A mutual affection begins to grow, and your mind begins
to change. Adjusting your mind to the realities of Scripture
becomes a focus. As this happens, you become a child again. I
cannot explain what happens when you give yourself to God.
In fact, I don't want to. That is an experience you need to have
with him. But what I can say is you will never be the same.

Intimacy builds through time and time alone. You cannot
build a relationship with anyone you don't spend time with. Ask
yourself for a moment, what do you spend time on? Who do
you spend time with? Where do your thoughts roam? Do you
gravitate toward positive or negative outcomes? When attacks
come, where do you run? The little girl in this story is me. She
is still my inner child. I still need her faith.

As you will see in the next chapters, the enemy, Satan, is after
the child in you. He is after your purity, your innocence, the way
you trust. He is out to break the bond you have with your heavenly Father. He wants you on your own. You are much easier to
defeat without Jesus. Childhood is essential to a healthy adulthood. Many times, people cannot trust because they did not

---

[5] Webster's 1828 American Dictionary of the English Language, Walking
Lion Press, West Valley City, UT, 2010.

have a good beginning. Countless people grew up in a violent, scary house with very little love and no acceptance. Children frequently are not loved as they should have been because of situations out of their control. One story of someone dear to me helped me realize just how real broken trust is.

When a young boy was around six years old, he began to climb a tree in his front yard. He was excited to finally climb the tree. Up and up he went until he reached the top. As he began to descend, he became scared. The reality of where he was became a bit much for him. He yelled for someone to rescue him. After some time, his father came to the front yard to see what all the yelling was about. He asked him, "How did you manage to get up there?" He was not happy with this young boy. The child yelled back, "I need some help, please. I can't get down." The father told him that he couldn't climb up to get him, so he was going to need to jump. The father guaranteed the child he would catch him. As the young boy jumped, the father moved out of the way, and the child hit the ground. The father looked at his son and said, "That should teach you never to trust anyone." I cannot explain why an adult would do that to a child. I don't even want to think about his reasons. To me, his reasons don't even matter. Regardless of why he chose to do that, he did. Maybe someone has dropped you too. Maybe someone dropped you today.

This is exactly why Satan uses people. He creates these roadblocks in our lives that are so big we cannot see how a heavenly Father would be any different. God is asking us to trust in him, someone we cannot see. How exactly are we supposed to do that? Unfortunately, this experience has plagued this man his whole life. Even though he knows God, he still can't trust people.

So now, I have this situation in my life that is too big for me. My friend's baby has leukemia. I am not a doctor. I cannot cure her. Now what? Time with Jesus is the answer. Time before this situation, in this situation, and after the situation is the cure. The cure is Jesus. The Word is medicine.

I head back outside. These thoughts of leukemia are torture for me. I agonize over this situation. I cry a lot! I know that Jesus is with me, this same Jesus who showed me the rocks, taught me about nature, and began to speak. "Mychelle, you know that there is a spiritual world bigger than this moment, a world you do not fully understand." As he removes my sadness, he creates a picture in my mind's eye. I see our baby in the middle of a circle. Jesus sits in the middle of the circle with our sweet little girl. She plays; he watches. As she plays, I realize that it isn't only Jesus present. The outer portion of this circle is knitted together by Christians who all believe in the power of Christ. Jesus is in each one of us. His power flows through all of us. Each member is a unique being with their own understandings and experiences with Jesus. The job of each one of these people is to keep watch over the baby, protecting her, speaking God's Word over her, and allowing no evil to reach her. God has purposefully placed these particular people in her life for such a time as this. John 15:5-8.

I am the Vine; you are the branches. When you're joined with me and I with you, the relationship is intimate and organic, the harvest is sure to be abundant. Separated, you can't produce a thing. Anyone who separates from me is deadwood, gathered up and thrown on the bonfire. But if you make yourselves at home with me and my words are at home with you, you can be sure that whatever you

*ask will be listened to and acted upon. This is how my
Father shows who he is—when you produce grapes, when
you mature as my disciples.*

Jesus is our connection through the Holy Spirit to the Lord.
The more time we spend with Jesus, the easier it becomes to ask
and trust God for things way beyond our imagination. Jesus
cares about whom we spend time with and what we spend
time doing. Scripture says if we make ourselves at home with
Jesus, our prayers will be heard and acted upon. John 15:7. Our
prayers will be heard and acted upon. Meditate on that thought;
our prayers will be heard and acted upon. Through our maturity,
the Lord is able to show who he is and brings us victory.

John 5:9–10: *"I've loved you the way my Father has loved me.
Make yourselves at home in my love. If you keep my commands,
you'll remain intimately at home in my love. That's what I have
done—kept my Father's commands and made myself at home
in his love."* I can honestly say that this is my life. Through all
of my life, I have been able to find my home in the love of the
Lord. My life changes when I purposely set aside time to be with
Jesus. Jesus loves us the way the Father loves him. Jesus came to
show us what real love looks like. He came to love us in a way
no human can. He came to be the life we need, the life only God
can provide. Jesus says, "You will remain intimately connected
to me as you study by word." Jesus will attach himself to us as we
follow his Word. Our obedience brings comfort and the ability
to make ourselves at home in the love of the Lord.

Jesus continues in John 15: 11-15

*I've told you about these things for a purpose that my joy
might be your joy and your joy wholly mature. This is my*

command: Love on another the way I loved you. This is the very best way to love. Put your life on the line for your friends. You are my friends when you do the things, I command you. I am no longer calling you servants because servants don't understand what their master is thinking and planning. No, I've called you friends because I've let you in on everything I've heard from the Father.

Jesus teaches us to develop our joy and put our lives on the line for our friends. The little girl realizes it's time to begin.

Her simple playtime with rocks has changed into the warfare of the future. Her rocks will now become a giant killer. In the simplicity of childlike faith grows an incredible strength. Strength is built from the joy and understanding of how much she is loved. Because of her intimacy with the Lord, his overwhelming joy surrounds her. Through the giggle of yesterday comes the solidity of today. Because she laughed and knows Jesus, she can stand now. Beyond her understanding comes an unmovable trust. Yes, her giggle becomes her rebel yell. She just giggles. She is happy.

As the demon called leukemia rears its ugly head, she takes her smooth stone and recalls the story of King David. A Philistine giant was threatening to take over the camp of the Israelites. Israel's army was frightened and had retreated. They had never seen a giant quite his size and were scared to attack him. The Philistines were threatening to kill the armies of Israel and take over their land. Someone needed to step up and demand victory. 1 Samuel 17:32–33: *"'Master,' said David, 'don't give up hope. I'm ready to go and fight this, Philistine.' Saul answered David, 'You can't go and fight this Philistine. You're too young and inexperienced—and he's been in this fighting business since before you were born.'"* I find this piece of Scripture interesting. God asks us to have childlike faith, and here David is being chastised for being so young. I am sure King Saul was afraid for David's life, especially as young and small as he was. What Saul didn't understand was the hours of time David had spent with God. David had spent many afternoons alone with the Lord.

1 Samuel 17:34–37:
David said, "I've been a shepherd, tending sheep for my father. Whenever a lion or bear came and took a lamb from the flock, I'd go after it, knock it down, and rescue the lamb. If it turned on me, I'd grab it by the throat, wring its neck, and kill it. Lion or bear, it made no difference—I killed it. And I'll do the same to this Philistine pig who is taunting the troops of God. God, who delivered me from the teeth of the lion and the claws of the bear, will deliver me from this Philistine."

Not only had David spent time with the Lord, but he had also watched the Lord kill bears and lions through his hands. He had more than an image of God; he knew God. He knew God would take care of him. He knew just how big his God was. As a child in the hands of God, David was growing into a king, all because he chose to spend time with the Father. *"Saul said, 'Go. And God help you.'"* I Samuel 17:37

In the next verses, Saul decided David should be dressed as a soldier to fight the giant. He tried to dress David in his armor. It's interesting that Saul was trying to dress a teenager in an adult's armor. The armor swallowed David. It was uncomfortable and too big. It certainly did not fit. What can we learn from this situation? You cannot live in someone else's armor.

You must develop your own relationship with the Lord. To be a soldier, you must allow God to teach you what he needs you to know. In 1 Samuel 17:39, David said, *"'I can't even move with all this stuff on me. I'm not used to this.' And he took it all off."* Instead, David searched for what he was familiar with. He looked for the things God had shown him; he searched for his rocks. His rocks were built on the trust he had in the Lord. The Philistine began to pace back and forth like a lion getting ready to attack. Satan takes this posture a lot. It is a posture of intimidation. He uses it to scare us. The Philistines began to tease David about his age. They wanted him to know they were not afraid of him. The Philistine jeered at David by telling him what he planned to do to him.

> *1 Samuel 17:45–47:*
> *David answered, "You come at me with sword and spear and battle-ax. I come at you in the name of GOD-of-the-Angel-Armies, the God of Israel's troops, who you curse and mock. This very day God is handing you over to me. I'm about to kill you, cut off your head, and serve up your body and the bodies of your Philistine buddies to the crows and coyotes. The whole earth will know that there's an extraordinary God in Israel. And everyone gathered here will learn that God doesn't save by means of sword or spear. The battle belongs to God—He's handing you to us on a platter."*

The battle belongs to the Lord. In situations that we do not understand nor really know how to fight, we need to remember the battle belongs to the Lord. I believe this is where we hide in the protection of the Most High. Although David's outward words were words of attack, his spirit was in the shelter of the Lord. His mouth yelled to the giant the words of victory, but his spirit was covered in the strength of God. God spoke the words of victory through David. David had a guarded hope. David's job was to trust God. David had to step out in faith, but the victory was already his. He understood his relationship with the Lord in such a way; he was not afraid of the pacing giant. David's confession was of the extraordinary God in Israel, not his own power. David understood fully his right as a child of God.

Once David proclaimed who would win the battle for him, the Philistine became incredibly angry and ran toward David to kill him. This is exactly who Satan is. He will run at you with everything he has when you quote Scripture to him. He hates you, and he hates God. When we speak God's Word into a situation, things may get worse for a time. He isn't going to quit. This is where the fight comes. Therefore it is so important to have spent time with the Lord. Imagine David standing there, and this giant is running toward him with all vigor and hate. What giant is running at you today? You have made a claim, have spoken God's words, and have believed in a miracle. All the sudden, the Philistine (Satan) begins to laugh. He charges. Now you must make a decision. What did David do? What will you do?

1 Samuel 17:48–50:
David took off from the front line, running toward the Philistine. David reached into his pocket for a stone, slung it, and hit the Philistine hard in the forehead, embedding the stone deeply. The Philistine crashed, face down in the dirt. That's how David beat the Philistine—with a

sling and a stone. He hit him and killed him. Not a sword for David!

As the demon called leukemia rears its ugly head, she takes her smooth stone and recalls the words of King David. It's time to take a giant's head off because she knows the battle belongs to the Lord. The same God who stood with David now stands with her. The battle is won. Through the intimacy and time, she has spent with Jesus, she no longer feels afraid. She isn't concerned about the giant; she knows the champion. Jesus has taken a small child and grown her into an inner champion. There are no questions, only declarations. There are no worries, only resolutions. Today she will be victorious. Wrapped in the umbrella of childlike faith is the most beautiful combination of strength and surrender, joy and war, and laughter and confidence. She may be the one throwing the stone, but God is hitting the target. It is time for rocks and giggles.

Try It:

1. Go for a walk and invite Jesus to join you.
2. Learn scripture.
3. Find your inner child again.

Scripture: He called a little child to him and placed the child among them. And he said: "Truly I tell you, unless you change and become like little children, you will never enter the kingdom of heaven. Therefore, whoever takes the lowly position of this child is the greatest in the kingdom of heaven. And whoever welcomes one such child in my name welcomes me" (Matt. 18:1–5).

6

"So, I let go of the cappuccino and released the word to her. It was very simple—I asked her permission first if I could share something encouraging with her. She said yes. I opened my mouth and said, "God really loves you. He has heard your cries, and He hasn't forgotten you, and He is going to heal and restore your family." —Lana Vawser[11]

You Are a Hannah

What Is the Cry of Your Heart?

Focus: She remembered who she was, and the game changed.

Focus: She advances in agreement that what she prayed shall be done because of God's partiality toward his daughter.

Scripture: So, Hannah ate. Then she pulled herself together, slipped away quietly, and entered the sanctuary. 1 Samuel 1:8

What God does through the cry of a woman is monumental. Women are spectacular beings. They are built for love, family, and nurture. Women care for and encourage the growth and development of their families for generations to come.

Fear was given a stage and was allowed to enter homes all over the world; FEAR, one of Satan's, the designated accuser's, biggest tactics.

In 2020, a virus spread, eating and creating havoc. It spread like a nasty fog. Its name, COVID-19. It came to kill, steal, and destroy. It was given reign to use its fingers to choke human necks, to take our very breath. It came to take life and, in the process, destroy livelihood. Fear spread, and leaders buckled. The threat and dread of the unknown created chaos and defeat. Neighbor turned on neighbor; love your neighbor no longer existed. Leadership blasted, "Stay away, be in isolation, and don't go out!" Schools closed, churches closed, and businesses closed. Quiet desperation roamed the streets. Simultaneously, Satan, the designated accuser, launched another strike to further separate people. Not only were people afraid of physical touch, but now color inequality was as lethal as the virus.

Authority was labeled and blamed for human actions. "Dismantle the police" was chanted on the streets and social media. In the middle of this confusion, children began to wonder if truth exists. People questioned God; they wondered where he went. In times of uncertainty and loneliness, the mind creates scenarios that can be painfully scary. Panic will kill hope and dreams and take our very breath. Suicide becomes an option.

The struggle is real and chronic. Trying to move past something you can't control is very difficult. Where is God?

For believers in Christ, we have hope. We also have a peace that surpasses all understanding. We have a Bible (the Word of God), the Holy Spirit, and our Savior, Jesus Christ. We must use the teachings from the Word of God to adjust our minds to the reality of Scripture. It's our own choice. Where we spend our time trains our minds, controls our words, and determines our outcomes. We must learn to allow our hearts to lead our minds. We either believe and obey the teachings of our father no matter the circumstances, or we don't. Plain and simple.

Is it okay to question, wonder, or ask? Absolutely, wisdom comes from deep intellect with God. Reading his Word and studying examples helps us make decisions. COVID-19 is a disease. Racial controversy is a human sentence. People without God are leading on the principle of emotions tied to self-preservation. Protecting themselves is the focus. Why? Because there are two sides: God, the father of love and grace, or Satan, the father of "I." There are no other choices.

People either love God or self. The manipulation of weak minds isn't difficult. Say what people want to hear, blame someone for your mistakes, and expect handouts. Once a person takes the handout, the next one better follow. It's easy to turn on the benefactor when needs aren't met. The justification for mean actions is easily accepted. Truth is replaced by emotional turmoil and reasoning. Small handouts are little reward in exchange for freedom.

Being a Christian can become a difficult task. The follower of Christ is asked to live above the snake line. In reclamation, a kiss on the cheek comes from our heavenly Father to keep us above the line. With that one kiss, our eyes can be opened, our hearts mended, and our lives protected. The kiss is waiting in the arms of the Most High.

Along with COVID-19, something happened to our family. Something other than my mother's death rocked me to my core. Something really scared me. My son was twenty-two at the time. He was living in Clovis and trying to discern where his life was heading. He made a mistake on Father's Day that could have shattered his life. He had a car accident that was his fault, an accident that caused a lot of damage and got worse over time.

One of the people in the accident was hurt, and we didn't find out until several days later just how bad his injury was. It is still difficult for me to discuss or write about, but I believe God is asking me to share this story because if we haven't gone through something similar yet, there is the probability at some point, we will—the fight with FEAR.

When you are a mother, your every happiness resounds in the happiness of your children. You watch over them like a hawk. You pray for them, love them unconditionally, and only want the best for them. Being a mom is the best reward and the hardest work. When your children make decisions that frighten you, worry you, or are not what you expect, then dealing with the fear of the consequences for them can become overwhelming. The actions of your children can become the worst nightmares you have ever experienced.

Trusting the Lord when your children are involved should be the easiest thing we do. In fact, what upset me the most about the accident was I knew better. I knew the Bible, I knew Scripture, and I knew the authority I have over his life. But the fear of the unknown and the consequences of his actions were staring me in the face. I was scared to death. I reacted poorly and wasn't handling the situation well at all. I was working in the flesh, not resting in the Spirit. I was blessed to be able to leave town, and that is exactly what I did.

I ran to the mountains. I ran to the highest shelter. I ran as fast as I could. I ran from the issue and into the only place I felt comfort. I ran to my Father. I brought beautiful friends and family who would encourage me in the Lord. I went to settle my spirit, seek God, and take action. I needed God, and he showed up.

Over the course of the next few days, I prayed, cried, and slept. I needed to claim victory. I needed to decree what I expected to see. I prayed earnestly for everyone involved to recover and their health restored.

What are you tied to emotionally? Take a few minutes to write down areas of your life that, if they are messed with, it takes time to find your footing: kids, family, business, spouse, career, finances, health, and so on.

John 8:23–24:
Jesus said, "You're tied down to the mundane (belonging to the world). I'm in touch with what is beyond your horizons. You live in terms of what you see and touch. I'm living on other terms. I told you that you were missing God in all of this. You're at a dead end. If you won't believe I am who I say I am, you're at the dead end of sins. You're missing God in your lives (emphasis added).

Consider what you wrote down at the top and place it next to the truth. Does this resonate with you? Do you understand how we do just that? You live in terms of what you see and touch.

Be honest. Are you missing God in your life? Maybe you are strong in some areas and others you need help. Maybe there is a root of rejection, abandonment, or bitterness locked away in your soul. If you won't believe I am who I say I am, you are at a dead end. That's why you don't see hope, you don't see an answer, why your emotions run with your life, and why you cry and won't sleep or eat. You are missing me in this situation, in every moment of your life, because of your unbelief.

Prayer: Lord, help us with our unbelief.

It is time to receive your kiss today. It is time to understand you are stronger than you know. Hold on and don't let go. You are going to be okay, and in the middle, you have the Holy Spirit to come alongside you, to pray with you, lift your head, and remind you of who you are. His voice is shouting, "Thunder coming, steadfast coming, boldness coming, and above all, victory is coming!" Are you ready to usher in his presence like never before? Be ready, get ready, and see the glory of our father, it is time!

The Lord knows every second of your life. He knows it all. He has walked through it all. He has never left. He has taken the hard questions following discouragement and has established every victory. He has set up a plan for your life. He knows your identity. He gave you your true name.

Zephaniah 3:17: "The Lord your God is in your midst, a mighty one who will save; he will rejoice over you with gladness; he will quiet you by his love; he will exult over you with loud singing."

How do we change our inner thought life? How do we not miss God in the middle of our emotions? STOP. Plain and simple. STOP your current thought process. Find your Bible and pray. You have to STOP the normal and build a new habit. "On average it takes more than two months before a new habit becomes automatic, sixty-six days to be exact," James Clear.[12]

In 1 Samuel 1:1–2, we are introduced to a woman by the name of Hannah. Hannah was married to Elkanah, and Elkanah had a second wife named Penninah. Penninah had children, but

Hannah did not. Each year the family traveled to Shiloh, where Elkanah would give sacrifices to the Lord. He sacrificed well on behalf of his family, but for Hannah, the sacrifice was doubled. He loved her very much and understood how much she wanted a child.

Many times, we are left without. Maybe we are left without a spouse, friends, family, money, health, and so on. The list goes on and on. Deep inside, we are wounded, afraid, and sad. Usually, we have someone who loves us, but at times, it may be hard to recognize it. Struggles are real.

However, in the middle of this sadness, there can be a double portion. Elkanah gave more than the requirement for his beautiful wife, Hannah. Let that sink in for a moment. It was more than the requirement. We have a Savior who gave more than the requirement; he gave his life. We have a father who gave his only Son to rescue us from the torment of this life.

This double portion did not come without taunting. In the middle of love and sacrifice stood the opposition, reminding Hannah in a most obvious way that she didn't have children. Peninnah reminded Hannah daily of what she didn't have. The Bible says she taunted her. A taunt*(s)*is a remark made to anger, wound, or provoke someone.[6] In this situation, I believe the purpose was to wound. Let's stop and take a few moments to write down the wounds we have. Take some time and think about the wounds you carry with you. Maybe they are deep-seated, and you carried them for years, or maybe it is just a situation you find yourself in. Wounds come in a variety of ways. They can be verbal, physical, mental, or seasonal. "*He was*

---

[6] Webster's 1828 American Dictionary of the English Language, Walking Lion Press, West Valley City, UT, 2010.

wounded for their transgressions, bruised for their iniquities. By his stripes, they are healed" (Isa. 53:5, emphasis added).

Wounds are a big deal and leave scars. We can heal from them, but the hurt often lingers, sometimes until we die. Wounds can happen in childhood and change our entire worldview. Others can come without notice. Some leave a hole in the middle of us. Peninnah taunted Hannah to continually remind her of what she wasn't, what she didn't have, and how she wasn't a real woman. Satan does that to us all. He wants to remind us of what we have lost, what we don't have, and who we are not.

Jesus bore wounds on his hands, feet, and in his side. His head was pierced with a crown of mockery. His back was fileted open with taunting lashes. Jesus placed all the hurt on himself in great agony. His agony replaced the wounds of our lives. Maybe it's time to hand him the battle scars; he paid a huge price to take them from us.

We need to give the Holy Spirit the time to whisper to us, speak to us, and listen to what he is saying. We need to remind ourselves of his love for us. We need to remind ourselves of how he sees us and what he thinks of us. We may be afraid of letting go of what has defined us because it is familiar. We know how to deal with our own thoughts, and when we begin to try and let go of them, the change can be almost too much. We have to begin to give him what we don't want and exchange it for who we are in him. Let his words begin to grow inside of us.

How did Hannah handle her sorrow? 1 Samuel 1:7: *"This went on year after year. Every time she went to the sanctuary of God she could expect to be taunted. Hannah was reduced to tears and had no appetite."* Year after year, she showed up in God's house only to be taunted. Year after year, she showed up to ask God to help her. Year after year, she left sad and depressed.

Finally, she just cried and didn't eat. We have all been in this place. We may not want to admit it to anyone, but we've been there. No matter what caused it, we've been there. We have all felt the sting year after year, the sting of no answers. In the middle of this torture, the sadness can be so hard to overcome that we don't eat, we don't sleep, and we cry all day. Do you have an appetite? What is your appetite for? We must become hungry for the Word of God, hungry for what he says about us, hungry for the bread of life.

1 Samuel 1 8–11: "*Her husband Elkanah said, 'Oh Hannah, why are you crying? Why aren't you eating? And why are you so upset? Am I not of more worth to you than ten sons?' So, Hannah ate. Then she pulled herself together, slipped away quietly, and entered the sanctuary.*" In *Steel Magnolias*[13], there is a scene after the death of a daughter. The mother, played by Sally Field, says that men are supposed to be made of steel or something. But the father left, and the husband left in the final moments of her daughter's life. She goes on to say how she stayed in the room and held her daughter's hand. She continues by saying she was with her daughter when she came into the world and was there when she drifted out. As a woman, she knows how lucky she is to be a mother.

No matter what we face, women have a way of pulling ourselves together and making a new start. We are resilient and steadfast. What did Hannah do first? She ate. She ate physical food. She restored her energy. We absolutely cannot stand up to Satan on an empty stomach. He comes when we are exhausted and depleted. The first thing we need to do is eat. We need to restore our energy source to be strong for our journey. Eat!

Secondly, her husband reminded her of what she had and how important she was to him. Who is in your corner? What do they speak over you to encourage you? Hang onto those words and allow them to pull you up. Focus on the promises. Through this reminder, Hannah pulled herself together and headed to the sanctuary. Once she ate, she got up, and she headed to the one place she knew she would get answers. She headed to see her Father.

Hannah went to the temple and cried inconsolably. She cried without ceasing. Her heart was so broken that she just poured it out to the Lord. Then she made a vow. 1 Samuel 1:11: *"Oh God of the Angel Armies, if you will take a good hard look at my pain, if you will quit neglecting me and go into action for me, by giving me a son, I'll give him completely, unreservedly to you. I'll set him apart for a life of holy discipline."* The priest, Eli, thought Hannah was drunk and told her to sober up. She was weeping so boldly the priest thought she was drunk. Hannah was in desperation. When Paden caused the car accident, I went into complete desperation. I wasn't eating. I cried a lot, and fear was so thick that I could feel it all over me. I was uncertain and afraid of what could happen to his life. The situation was completely out of my control.

I had to make time for the Holy Spirit to whisper to me and listen to what he was saying. In these situations, we must remind ourselves of his love for us and what he thinks of us. We may be afraid of letting go of what defines us, but that is exactly what we need to do. In our humanity, we will make decisions that, in a spur of a moment, may change our lives forever. We live in a scary world filled with other humans who also have free will. We live in uncertainty and mistakes. The overcoming of mistakes can take a lifetime. Even when we have studied the Bible, we can still fall into unbelief and fear. It doesn't mean we don't love the Lord; it just means the reality of situations can be overwhelming.

The only thing we can do is read Scripture and consume ourselves with the authority we have in Christ. I cannot imagine what it must be like to not have God in the middle of uncontrollable circumstances. The idea of handling life without God to help me scares me more than whatever comes against me. God is the creator. He sees the future. He never leaves me. Without the Lord, there is only what we make humanly possible. There is no divine intervention. Confusion and reasoning don't help in situations out of our control. Peace only comes when you can hand the circumstance over to the one who can truly make a difference.

Often when situations are out of our control, we make inner vows. If we are in an abusive situation, an inner vow could be, "Once I am free, no one will ever hurt me again." Or "I'll never trust a man again." Inner vows can be life-altering. By definition, a vow(s) is a promise made to God or a duty. [7] Let that sink in. When you make an inner vow, it's either to the Lord or the devil. Yes, inner vows carry a significant amount of power. A vow is a promise to do something following a particular event.

Hannah made a vow to God. My son's accident occurred in the middle of writing this book. So, it's not like I didn't know what to pray, confess, or believe. I knew plenty. But because of the damage I saw, the damage I heard of, and the uncertainty of the consequences, I panicked! On top of my fear, Satan tried to make me feel guilty for being afraid. He challenged my walk with God and threatened the life of my child and those in the

[7] Webster's 1828 American Dictionary of the English Language, Walking Lion Press, West Valley City, UT, 2010.

accident. He created a death trap and drove my son right into it. He comes to kill, steal, and destroy.

So, how do we stop this mudslide of painstaking thoughts? Get away from it. Surround yourself with believers. Make bold statements built on Scripture. Give God the problem. Cast away the thoughts. Cry. Take the issue directly to the Lord. Physically symbolize what needs to happen.

In this case, I headed to the mountains with true believers. I spoke my heart, asked for prayer, cried my eyes out, studied the Word, decreed the outcome, and threw rocks into the river as a symbol of letting go. I was absolutely leaving my fear in the river with my promise in tow. The cry of a woman about her child moves the heavens. God honors our love.

1 Samuel 1:16: *"The only thing I've been pouring out is my heart, pouring it out to God. Don't for a moment think I am a bad woman. It's because I am so desperately unhappy and in such pain that I stayed here so long."* Desperately unhappy and in great pain—no one ever wants to be here. But we all face situations, which leave us desperately unhappy and full of pain. I believe Hannah's story was written for me and all women. I believe her story mirrored my story. I believe we are sisters desperate for God to intervene with our children. I believe if the Lord heard her prayer, then he will hear mine. She remembered who she was, and the game changed.

Hannah's desperation brought her to a place of action. She went to the temple on her own and boldly prayed to the only one who could change her situation. She was determined. Although her heart was heavy, she believed. She had the expectancy that God would change her situation. Do you have that bold confidence? Are you willing to promise or vow to the Lord what you are willing to do if He will move on your behalf? Hannah promised the Lord she would separate this child for His service. Are we willing to sacrifice amid our promise? Jesus did.

1 Samuel 1:17-18: "Eli answered, *'Go in peace. And may the God of Israel give you what you have asked him.' 'Think well of me and pray for me,'* she said. She went on her way. Then she ate heartily, her face radiant" (emphasis added). She knew her answer was coming. That night, she conceived a child.

What are we learning?

It is okay to cry. It is okay to come in desperation. It is okay to boldly ask God for answers. It is okay to make a vow to God. It is okay to expect answers to prayer. It is okay to leave all your anxiety with him. It is okay to eat and move prayer into action.

It is important to read the next verses of Hannah's story because she teaches us how to give glory to God when he works the miracle we have asked for. 1 Samuel 1:20: *"She named her child Samuel, explaining, 'I asked God for him.'"* Hannah brings Samuel back to the temple and shows him to Eli. She dedicates him to the Lord, fulfilling the vow she made, and she worshiped the Lord for him. She prays once again, honoring and thanking God for what He did in her life.

Hannah's second prayer is her thankful heart. When God comes through for us and shows himself faithful, we need to recognize and give him all the glory. God deserves our love and gratitude. Mark things down and write them on the fabric of your heart. Tell others of your victories. God is always at work on our behalf, and when your answer comes, share your story!

Because of God's greatness, everyone in the accident recovered. Paden learned a lesson. I have a testimony!

I learned that just like Hannah, God heard my cry, fear, and desperation, and He answered on all of my accounts. Even when Satan taunts, situations are dangerous, and you feel sad and depressed, there is a God who puts people on their feet again. He rekindles burned-up lives with fresh hope. He has all operations on earth on firm foundations.

Try It:

1. Talk with God.
2. Pray boldly.
3. Give God praise.

Scripture: Numbers 6:22–26: "God spoke to Moses: 'Tell Aaron and his sons, this is how you are to bless the People of Israel.' Say to them, 'The Lord bless you and keep you; the Lord make his face shine on you and be gracious to you and give you peace.'"

7

"Why? Because I told my kids there was nothing in the dark to be afraid of. I am making sure it stays that way."
—An American Soldier[14]

Our Victory Song

Who Can You Trust to Follow?

Focus: Our prayer is our victory.

Scripture: "Our Father in heaven, hallowed be your name. Your kingdom come, your will be done, on earth as it is in heaven. Give us this day our daily bread, and forgive us our debts, as we also have forgiven our debtors. And lead us not into temptation but deliver us from evil" (Matt. 6:9–13).

Mysteries are not often welcomed. The unknown can be a dark place. The unknowns in life seem to outweigh the known. The mind searches for the next thing in life: college tuition, retirement, final homes, heritage, and legacy. The building of life has been built; the legacy is what matters now. Uncertain economic times and disunity among the states has created a very volatile and unstable environment. The thought of an outside attack lingers. Where is America? Where has she gone? What was she founded on? How has she made it this long? What is the responsibility of a Christian?

Freedom always comes at a price. We hear the saying soldiers lay down their lives for their countries. It isn't a saying; it is the truth. Many soldiers lay down their lives for people they have never met or for people who are not even born. They choose to serve because freedom is important to them. They believe in a cause much greater than themselves. Their names may never be known, but they died for a purpose, a reason. Servanthood is a narrow and often unnoticed pathway. For every sin, there is a sacrifice.

Servant, sacrifice, and freedom; interesting how these three words go together when describing a soldier. Currently in America, these three words are creating a barrier between races and gender. But to a soldier, they coincide with peace and purpose. How do these three words reflect in the heart of a Christian? Where does God take us on this journey? Do they bring peace and purpose, or do they create barriers and fear?

In our hearts, where does our father God lay? What is his purpose, sacrifice, and freedom? What do those three words mean for a believer? I wonder if there is a level we haven't reached yet, a level that God is trying to show us that our worldly minds have such difficulty understanding. What is my responsibility in a relationship with God, and what is he wanting me to understand? Our minds are the battlefield, and as soldiers, how do we win the war? Going into battle cannot be our focus without training. Life's training is up and down, positive, and negative, and victory and defeat. How can I live in the peace and victory Jesus left even if the outside circumstance is beyond my control?

War movies are not a genre I choose on a regular basis. However, I live in a house of three men, so they enjoy the entire spectrum of history and war-based movies. The other day, Mitchell was watching a movie starring Tom Hanks about war ships that were used to safely deliver supply boats during World War II. I didn't watch much of it, but I did pick up on several ideas. First, the battle was intense, and it was the initial outing for the captain. As the movie opened, the captain prayed for the Lord to be with him and guide him and his crew. It didn't take long before war was at his front door. They were being attacked by Russian submarines.[15]

Many concepts flowed through my mind as I heard Tom Hanks, as the captain, know what to do and give orders to those around him. I realized his authority was "the" authority. The crew was a complete unit. They didn't question or reason the captain's decisions; they simply followed his lead. The captain trusted his men to follow his commands and give him advice. They worked cohesively together. The attacks didn't cease. In fact, they became more focused, more clever, and more frequent. The positioning of the enemy changed, as did his tactics. The battle was intense and damaging. The crew's resolve never changed. They had three purposes: service, freedom, and sacrifice.

There was a man many years ago who had a team. He was the leader, and he was the authority. He gathered a group of young men to change the world. He was the son turned servant who became the sacrifice for all to have freedom from sin. His name was Jesus. I have had the privilege of walking with Jesus for most of my life. I have always known him. I have always loved him. But at times, I don't think I have always obeyed him.

As I have grown up, I have tried to find my way in trusting the Lord and not being so concerned with things I can't control.

Being a mom is the most blessed job in the world but also the most frightening. There are so many things in my boys' lives that I don't have any control over. I am not sure where the fear was allowed to settle in my life, but it became incredibly present in the year 2020.

Fear and panic settled deep in my soul following a car accident my son had. It took several days for me to let it go. He and everyone involved are okay, but there was a week of uncertainty that just about devoured my life. What I want to discuss is what was going on in my mind after the accident. FEAR! There were loud and booming thoughts of all kinds of situations, ideas, and consequences. I was in a very bad place. I spent time with some dear family and friends in which they had to help me fight demonic battles I had never encountered before.

I was in a battle. I had my crew. I needed a captain . . . I knew Jesus, I was writing a book about him. But in this uncertain and horrific time, I wasn't seeing him. I wasn't seeing clearly. I wasn't putting Scripture into my life. It was like I knew what I should be doing, but the pain and intensity of my thought life was so overwhelming that I wasn't able to pull myself out of it. I went through intense therapy with those around me. I am forever grateful for the five people God himself sent into my life for such a time.

I began to understand that I knew a lot and had studied a lot, but I need to learn how to trust a lot. The reality of writing this book is the actual understanding that I need to know how much God loves me and that he will never leave me. In fact, through the course of writing this book, the Lord spoke to me and said, "When you actually believe everything you are writing about, that is when your life will change." I think I believed certain things shouldn't happen to me or my family because God was supposed to prevent all bad things from happening. I don't know that I purposely thought that, but I do know I was taught to make good decisions and that God would reward those. I had a mixed-up teaching when I was little. I was taught that my actions were a big part of my relationship with God. I wasn't taught much about grace and didn't see the Lord as a captain fighting for my survival.

So now, at age fifty-one, what do I do to teach myself about the areas I fall short in? I start over, become a child again, and think about being born again. Spiritual maturity is essential, and we should grow up with the Lord, but growing up isn't about giving more lectures, being able to counsel others, or writing a book. Spiritual maturity is being able to fight Satan at every turn and not allowing him to rent space in your head but being able to trust God in every situation. Being mature is giving God complete control and remaining at peace because of it.

Therefore, I need a starting place. I need to be able to change my thoughts and my life. I need Scripture to be my reality. I pondered these needs and began to ask God where to begin. I had done this before, but this time it was different. I needed God in a different way. I needed a breakthrough. I didn't want to return to the place I was after the accident.

I find it almost so simple that it's hard to believe. God led me to the Lord's Prayer, a prayer I had prayed from the time I was very small, before every basketball game. One I didn't take very seriously. Now, that isn't a good thing to admit, but I had prayed this prayer so many times in so many small situations, but I didn't understand its power. I believe this is a danger for Christians. Do we know so much of the Word that we don't really use or believe it? Do we take for granted the power in the Word of God simply because we have heard it so many times?

God was calling me to dig deep, to become a follower of him like I have never followed before.

"Our Father in heaven, hallowed be your name. Your kingdom come, your will be done, on earth as it is in heaven. Give us this day our daily bread, and forgive us our debts, as we also have forgiven our debtors. And lead us not into temptation but deliver us from evil" (Matt. 6:9–13). As we begin to unpack this prayer, consider how its words are used in so many different places throughout Scripture. These words will be referenced in many places. This isn't a quick study. Each line is significant and should take time to chew and savor.

"Our Father in heaven, hallowed be your name."

Our Father, the one who feeds and protects us. He feeds us through his words. His Son is the bread of life. He protects us through the understanding and application of his Word into the situation. He gives us proactive stances to send forth his Word, to decree his promises in our lives. God is the father of all men. He is the author, creator, and inventor of our faith. He is the father of spirit and light. He is our protector, defender, and the great I AM. He comes first, and he adopts us into his family. He provides a way to him through his Son, Jesus, the Christ. As his children, we are free to run to him, love him, ask him questions, and feel safe under his wings. He is the first, the last, and everything in between. When we pray to him, he listens and works on our behalf. His name is holy, powerful, reverent, and strong. It should be spoken with respect and recognized for its power. Every time we think of him, we should understand and fear his great and mighty strength and ability to sustain life. There is no other than our Father, the Lord of the universe. Obeying his laws brings victory; ignoring his commands brings conse-quences. He is holy, and we must obey his set laws for this world. As his child, you get to pray to the God who owns all, knows all, loves all, and can change history. You get to pray to the only one who can stop time and make the impossible possible! This father will never leave you.

"Your kingdom come, your will be done, on earth as it is in heaven."

God brought heaven to earth through his Son, Jesus. He sent his Word in human form so we might taste and see. John 1:14: *"The word became flesh and blood and moved into the neighbor-hood"* (emphasis added). *"Come and see"* (John 1:46, emphasis added). God's kingdom reigns above earthly kingdoms. He is a king, but he isn't brutal and mean. A kingdom is a government. It is the authority among the land. God's creative power formed the earth and all it holds. He had a perfect plan for the humans he gave control of the planet to. It was through man's sin that things changed. When we pray for his kingdom to come, we are praying for God's original intent for our planet to become the reality we see. His original intent was perfection. There was no sickness, murder, deceit, or ungodly behavior. We were to choose to follow and love him as much as he loved us.

When we believe in Jesus and pray through the Holy Spirit, our hearts change how we see things. We can pray for his will to be done on earth as it is in heaven because we understand the change that needs to come. We begin to understand what is allowed in heaven and what is not; therefore, we can ask for our earthly walk to look more like heaven then a defeated planet. We are asking God to invade our earthly life and mirror it to heaven.

God set up the tree of knowledge, which represented the good and bad of free will, and he wanted Adam and Eve to trust him and not eat of the fruit. But the serpent was crafty and tricked Eve into eating the fruit, changing human outcomes forever. See Genesis 3. But we can bring heaven into our daily lives through praying for it to happen. In John 3:5–6, Jesus was speaking with a leader, Nicodemus. Jesus was teaching Nicodemus the need to be born again. *"Unless a person submits to this original creation—'wind hovering-over-the-water' creation, the invisible moving the visible, a baptism into a new life—it's not possible to enter God's kingdom."* We must submit our lives fully to God first. He has to be the one and only authority. Our will must be submitted to his Lordship.

In life, circumstances occur. Certain circumstances bring certain responses out of us. Our emotions are a big part of our reactions, questions, and decisions. When confronted with things we don't like, we can become irrational, bitter, frustrated, or standoffish. Jesus wants us to let go of our natural tendencies and look to him for our understanding and actions. In John 3:11, Jesus continued to speak with Nicodemus, *"There is nothing second hand here, no hearsay. Yet instead of facing the evidence and accepting it, you procrastinate with questions. If I tell you things that are plain as the hand before your face and you don't believe me, what use is there telling you of things you cannot see, the things of God?"* Questions arise, and we want to know why things happened. God doesn't mind our questions if they don't lead us down the path of unbelief or procrastination. Jesus is simply saying, trust me.

"Give us this day our daily bread."

Take time to chew. Sweet, warm, and fulfilling is the bread of life. The disciples were on a journey with Jesus. Not everything made sense to them at first. Not everything happened according to their plans. In some cases, it was after Jesus rose from the dead that they fully understood his message. That's why we must take time to chew on what he says. We are on a journey too. God's words are "now" words. Come and see.

The Lord gave us Communion. The word *communion(v)* means the sharing or exchanging of intimate thoughts and feelings, especially when the exchange is on a mental or spiritual level. [8] Not only did Jesus want to share his most intimate thoughts and feelings with us, but he also laid his life down for us. He covered us with his blood and his body. Jesus refers to himself as the bread of life and the light of the world. And through Communion, he gives himself over completely to us. We are able to become like him. We can taste heaven. We are protected among the wolves. He left nothing undone. Our daily bread is Jesus. When we ask for God to give us this day our daily bread, we are asking him to give us all of Jesus. We are asking for Jesus to be present and the Holy Spirit to guide us in all our decisions. Asking for his presence at the beginning of the day keeps us out of trouble.

"And forgive us our debts, as we also have forgiven our debtors."

What is forgiveness? Why is it so crucial? How does God view unforgiveness? Satan, who, at one time, was created as a

---

[8] Webster's 1828 American Dictionary of the English Language, Walking Lion Press, West Valley City, UT, 2010.

blameless cherub, is now the demon accuser. He is also called the father of lies. He doesn't ring your doorbell and ask to take a seat on your couch and accuse you of all sorts of things. He doesn't stand in line and wait his turn. No, he comes to your Father in the courts of heaven, and he uses every mistake you have ever made to keep the love of God from you. He points his fingers as you. He raises his voice. He lays out every sin you have committed, and he tells God to keep you out of heaven, not bless you, and your punishment should be death. He wants you out of God's grace. He uses anything he can to remove God's love from you. He despises you!

In the courtroom, God sits on his throne. He listens to what the accuser says. Then he looks at me or you and determines what he will judge us on. He does judge us. But here is the provision: you and I, if we have asked Jesus into our hearts, are covered in the blood of Jesus. So as God turns his head and looks at you, he only sees what his Son did. He only sees the blood. He judges us clean because Jesus is clean.

So why then is forgiveness important? What does the Scripture say? *"And forgive us our debts, as we also have forgiven our debtors."* God sits in the courtroom of our eternity and listens to an accuser who has plenty of ammunition in his favor to keep us from the love of God. But as he talks and shuffles around the courtroom, God sees us through the blood of his son. No matter how loud the devil yells, his voice falls on deaf ears. God does not make his decisions on the accusations. He makes them on his forgiveness based on our acceptance of his son.

I have been forgiven. You have been forgiven. We are to forgive others as we also forgive our debtors. This is part of how Jesus taught us to pray. If he specified forgiveness in our prayer to the Lord, he is serious about us doing it. Sometimes depending on the severity of the hurt, we will reason our behavior. For example, I had a supervisor I thought the world of. She was brilliant, beautiful, educated, and articulate. For a long time, I wanted to be just like her. She had authority and favor. She could get a job done, and people went to her for solutions. I liked her clothes, her car, and her spirit.

One day I was offered what I considered to be my dream job. I was able to work right underneath her. I was second in command, and I liked the position. At first, our relationship was completely amazing, and we achieved a lot. We were on the same page as we moved the school forward. We knew what we wanted and weren't afraid to make it happen. We were bold, authoritative, and goal driven. We accomplished a lot until things changed. Sometimes two is two too many. Over the next two years, our relationship became strained, and I left the job I thought would change my life forever, a job I never expected to leave.

But when I left, I left with a tremendous amount of hurt and rejection. She stayed, and I watched the school continue to be blessed. I struggled with the blessings of the school. I struggled with the coverage in the paper. I struggled with the financial blessings. I struggled with seeing her or being in the same church with her. Why? Because I reasoned in my mind that she had mistreated me. And maybe she had. But the unforgiveness in my heart toward her made me miserable. I told myself I had forgiven her, but every time I saw her, I realized I hadn't.

Whether or not she hurt me was a perception I had in my mind. Sometimes people are mean to us. Sometimes we think they are mean to us. Either case, what we believe is reality to us. I had a problem with loss, a problem deep-seated inside of me.

My mind would run wild with thoughts of rejection based on others' behaviors. It took the Lord revealing to me what the root of this thought process was in order to overcome it.

People will trespass against us. People will disappoint us. People will hurt us. People are messy and human. People have free will. Unless we want to live in a cave with no one around, we better understand the importance of forgiveness. I remember saying, "Well I have forgiven her, but it will take me a long time to trust people again." You see, when you begin to withdraw from others because of a single hurt somewhere else, you are shutting people out before they are even given a chance. If you have an argument and then keep them at bay, you are missing out on what they can bring to your life. You are going to have arguments. But God forgives, and he forgives again. We must find a way to let people out of the snare.

Forgiveness is non-negotiable. One day in my backyard, I asked God to help me fully forgive. I believe it was because I wanted approval so much that I created thoughts of rejection in my mind. I needed God to help me. And when I finally asked without hesitation, I heard what I thought was a tree falling. There was such a loud sound that I looked around to see where the tree hit the ground. The tree of unforgiveness had fallen. My heart was lighter. Father forgive them for they know not what they do. I called her and asked to begin a new friendship with her. We have a good relationship now. We probably won't ever work together again, and that is okay, but at least now I am happy for her blessings in life. I hope we will always have a friendship.

"And lead us not into temptation but deliver us from evil."

Temptation is a strong desire to do something, usually in regard to choosing to follow after God or the world. Our flesh, the devil, and the world offer a lot of choices that do not align to the Word of God. The Lord left us in the world to be a light for others to follow. He needs us to represent him on earth so that others may believe in him. In fact, as Jesus neared the end of his life, he prayed for all of us.

Jesus Prays for All Believers (John 17:20–23)

My prayer is not for them alone. I pray also for those who will believe in me through their message, that all of them may be one, Father, just as you are in me and I am in you. May they also be in us so that the world may believe that you have sent me. I have given them the glory that you gave me, that they may be one as we are one— I in them and you in me—so that they may be brought to complete unity. Then the world will know that you sent me and have loved them even as you have loved me.

Jesus is covering us in who he is with God. When Jesus says, "deliver us from evil," he prays that all of his believers are in him and the Lord. He specifically asks for us to be in complete unity with the Lord and himself. This prayer can help us stay away from evil as the world tempts us to taste it. The unique thing about becoming a Christian is that you are never alone. You have been given all characteristics of Jesus and learn how to become more like him daily. You are given the peace of Jesus and the Holy Spirit to lead and guide you. If you stop and take time to listen, Jesus always has the way. He is the light of the world, the hope of glory, and the victor. He hopes for a relationship with you. You have a team, you have a captain, you have a prayer, and there is nothing in the dark to be afraid of.

Try It:

1. Go for a walk.
2. Pray the Lord's Prayer over your life.
3. Forgive.

Focus: Our prayer is our victory.

Scripture: "Our Father in heaven, hallowed be your name. Your kingdom come, your will be done, on earth as it is in heaven. Give us this day our daily bread, and forgive us our debts, as we also have forgiven our debtors. And lead us not into temptation but deliver us from evil" (Matt. 6:9–13).

8

"You may be older in age, but you are about to take your place in the next step of your destiny on earth as you stay close to Him and His heart and listen to His voice."

—Lana Vawser[16]

Spiritual Acuity

Do You Have a Keen Spirit?

Focus: Thank you, Lord, for developing my sharpness or keenness of thought, vision, hearing, and range.

Scripture: All this I have spoken while still with you. But the Advocate, the Holy Spirit, who the Father will send in my name, will teach you all things and will remind you of everything I have said to you. Peace I leave with you; my peace I give you. I do not give to you as the world gives. Do not let your hearts be troubled and do not be afraid. John 14:25-27

Making life decisions is never easy. Sometimes following your heart isn't easy. At times, a simple "yes" may mean "no" to a lot of other things. What do you do when you are middle-aged, fifty-one, and you are ready for new beginnings? Settling is something most of us do. We settle into our lives. We have built homes, families, careers, and routines. Financially, we are solid or have our debt managed. So, why do some people need to "swing for the fence," so to speak? Why do some pastors build new churches at sixty? Why do some people need to take on difficult schools at sixty-two? Why do some people need to attain a doctorate degree at fifty? I believe it's because God places a desire for movement within us. There is a burning to test God with impossibility and see what he will do. For some, moving with God is the only life they know.

I have watched and listened to Joyce Meyer for thirty-plus years. Through this daily time with her, I feel like I know her. God gave me Joyce to help me through my mom's death, and she became like a second mom once my mom went to be with Jesus. Even though I have never met Joyce, she has inspired and disciplined my life daily. Why, at age seventy-eight, does Joyce continue the way she does? She has a calling. She has a gift. She has a purpose.

God calls us all into his ministry for his purposes. Some of us are teachers, some are encouragers, some are prophets, and so on. He needs all of us to use our talents for his kingdom. How do we "let go and let God?"

Heart motivation is the fuel for movement. Time with God develops the path we should take. Discussion with people we trust builds our faith. Bible study develops spiritual acuity. We cannot live life one without the other. God prepares us in multiple avenues to build our trust in Him. He will be silent at times to cause us to dig deep to find Him, not to hurt us but to solidify our understanding. To take a risk, you need to know the hand of God is gently placed on your back, nudging you forward. At the age of fifty, I decided to complete a book, write a curriculum for a college, and leave a twenty-seven-year public education career. I had many worries and fears. By trait, I am a worrisome and incredibly responsible person. I do not make rash decisions. I tend to overthink situations, beat myself up for mistakes, and worry about money. By no means am I a bungee jumper. I have spent a lot of time with God in the wilderness, about four years, to be exact. Four years prior to leaving public education, I was restless. I was tired, my passion was diminishing, I was frustrated, and financially stuck. We needed my salary. I had one son in vocational school and another starting high school. I wasn't sure of my next steps, but my soul was becoming tormented.

I knew I was getting ready for a change, only I didn't know what the change was. Being a planner, I didn't like the uneasiness of not knowing. It really bothered me. I would cry out to God. All I would hear was, "Read this Scripture," or "Study this book in the Bible." There were no career answers or direct vision. I spent time in the wilderness listening, writing, and studying.

Until one day . . .

God directly spoke to me about studying Exodus. He told me to study the book. He was bold as He encouraged my spirit to study, not read. My best advice is to study, not read. Through my study, the tenth chapter of this book, "Don't Be Afraid of No," came about. Rejection and loss had become roots in my life; roots that needed removing. Through understanding Moses's journey, I learned God already knows the rejection is coming, even before he allows us or sends us to go. Whether it is a job interview, a loss of a business, or a financial scare, God isn't surprised. He purposefully prepares us, and if we will listen, he teaches us lessons that change our lives. The Trinity involves three beings: God the Father, God the Son, and God the Holy Spirit. The Holy Spirit is often overlooked. And yet, he is the most influential in our everyday lives. God is in heaven, and Jesus sits at his right hand. The Holy Spirit moves among us and within us. He is the voice of God in our lives. In John 14, Jesus was preparing his disciples for his death. He was preparing them for a life without him on earth. Verses 25–27:

> *All this I have spoken while still with you. But the Advocate, the Holy Spirit, who the Father will send in my name, will teach you all things and will remind you of everything I have said to you. Peace I leave with you; my peace I give you. I do not give to you as the world gives. Do not let your hearts be troubled and do not be afraid.*

An advocate*(s)*, according to the dictionary, in its primary sense, signifies one who pleads the cause of another in a court of civil law. [9] Lawyers are considered advocates. Why would Jesus define the Holy Spirit as someone who defends us in court? Because God reigns in heavenly courts. His court is the highest court. Advocates are usually appointed by kings, governments, or militaries. The Holy Spirit is appointed by the kingdom to defend, dispense benefits, lead, protect revenue, defend churches, administer justice, give counsel, vindicate, plead favor for, claim us to be his own, and call us into action.

Jesus was sent to earth for us to see with our own eyes the mysteries of heaven. He continually said, "IF you have seen me, you have seen the father who sent me." Jesus laid down a pattern

---

[9] Webster's 1828 American Dictionary of the English Language, Walking Lion Press, West Valley City, UT, 2010.

for us as to what our lives should look like. He sent the Holy Spirit so we could understand God for ourselves, so we could seek the Lord in a whole new way. When a situation arises, the hope is that we bring it to the Lord and pray for the Holy Spirit to claim us as his own and teach us how to handle it. Our job is to ask him for favor and discernment. We should ask for the Holy Spirit to lead us to the right Scripture and help us believe in the promise. He helps our faith grow. We don't walk alone. We don't need to figure everything out. We don't have to lose our peace. We have an advocate who stands ready to plead our case to God, defend our minds and bodies, direct us into all wisdom, and give us the courage to step out in faith. John 15:26–27: "*When the Advocate comes, whom I will send to you from the Father—the spirit of truth who goes out from the father—he will testify about me. And you also must testify, for you have been with me from the beginning.*" Through the Holy Spirit, we learn truth that sets us free, the truth we should share with others. Acts 2: "'*In the Last Days,*' God says, '*I will pour out my Spirit on every kind of people: Your sons will prophesy, also your daughters; your young men will see visions, your old men will dream dreams. When the time comes, I'll pour out my spirit on those who serve me, men and women both.*'"

Acts 9:31: "*The Church enjoyed a time of peace and was strengthened. Living in fear of the Lord and encouraged by the Holy Spirit, it increased in numbers.* (Peter raised a woman from the dead. You will do greater things than I when the power of the Holy Spirit comes upon you.)"

Whosoever will.

There is an opportunity for every believer in Christ to understand God and experience his goodness to the level they are willing to seek, obey, sacrifice, and commit to. God wants to enable us to prophesy and watch his promises become reality. He wants to give us visions and dreams of what is to come, who we are in him, and our authority in this world. He wants to pour out his spirit on us. He wants to saturate you in everything he is, does, knows, and promises. In Matthew 7:24, Jesus said:

These words I speak to you are not incidental additions to your life, home-owner improvements to your standard of living. They are foundational words to build a life on. If you work these words into your life, you are like a carpenter who built his house on solid rock. Rain poured down, the river flooded, a tornado hit- but nothing moved the house. It was fixed to the rock.

Building 2020 vision or spiritual acuity in the Word develops a keen sense of the Lord. The more we read, study, believe, and apply, the more we will watch the Word work in our lives. The difference is our heart's motivation. Do we seek God as a home improvement? Or do we seek God as our foundation? Do we want him to fix our situations, or do we want to commit our lives to his Lordship? What you fill your heart and mind with is essential to who you will become. God, the creator of the universe, wrote the race of your life. Distractions come in the form of mindsets, circumstances, and strongholds. Place every thought captive and bring it to the submission of the hand of God.

When you are handed the baton, what will your leg of the race look like? God, the creator of the universe, wrote your race. Begin to see your bloodline as the great exchange for humanity. Jesus ran his race while keeping a dove firmly planted on his shoulder, Holy Spirit peace.

What if God kept an account in heaven and we were expected to pay a balance? What if he kept a tab on your deposits and withdrawals? Could you, on your own merit, pay for your place in heaven? And yet, day after day, we sit with the gold substance, the life-giving Word of God on a table, and think, "I'll get to it later." What can you afford to get to later? What do you depend on to save your life? Jesus paid the ultimate price for each of us. He paid with his life.

King Jesus is your coach; he placed you in a relay, and he gave you the victory.

YOU FIGHT FROM A PLACE OF VICTORY.

- Your eternity is settled.
- You're a son or daughter in God's kingdom.
- You stand in complete justice.
- You are clothed in victory.
- Your words are filled with spirit and truth.
- You have all authority.
- You're filled with the fruit of the spirit.
- You battle from a victory standpoint—not the standard of defeat.

But what happens when you don't see things from that perspective? In life, there is: loss, fatigue, fear, weariness, destruction, and death.

Allow yourself to heal, cry, scream, lose it, and completely fall apart. But also remember, you must get up. To be an overcomer, you must train. Train before you ever run a race. Train as if your life depends on it. Because the truth is, your life does depend on it.

1 Corinthians 9:26 (MSG):
I don't know about you, but I'm running hard for the finish line. I'm giving it everything I've got. No sloppy living for me! I'm staying alert and in top condition. I do not fight like a boxer beating the air. I'm not going to get caught napping, telling everyone else all about it and then missing out myself.

Are you a competitor?

In 2021, my niece became the third leg on a four by four hundred relay. She was a freshman in the giant state of Texas. I watched a young girl of fifteen become a state champion. During this period, she sacrificed every single day to be a part of something much bigger than herself. She was surrounded by older, confidant, and experienced girls. She listened as they trained her how to run a four hundred. She was talented and quick, but her determination, loyalty, and obedience are what won a gold medal.

In the verse above, it states, I'm running hard for the finish line. The Lord wants us in the race, and he wants us victorious. Life takes everything you've got. It takes time, competitiveness, resolve, understanding, courage, discipline, and love.

To develop your inner champion, you must believe a champion lives on the inside of you. You must understand what Jesus did on the cross, and who is with you every single day. You must be willing to obey his voice and not be sloppy in your choices. You need to be in top condition to box the accuser. He is coming for you and everyone you love. You must know the word, trust the word, rely on the word, and obey the word.

My beautiful young niece set a goal of running the quarter in under sixty seconds. She started the year at sixty-two. Her target was always sixty and she worked toward it every day. She began to train. She trained by running longer sprints, she trained by running short sprints, she trained by limiting her food intake, and she trained by running in multiple meets. Every Saturday was a test to see how close she was getting to meeting her sixty second run. Every Saturday was her gauge for her own goal. We live in a world full of tests. You are in training each day. You are either proactive and working the word into your life, or your reactive and praying God will take care of situations.

Training for a Christian is based on the work of the Holy Spirit in us. He is responsible for guiding us and teaching us. He will help us defeat our strongholds of doubt and build our faith in God. Our responsibility is to know the word and simply believe it. No matter the circumstance, you can be victorious. You can live a life Jesus died to give you. You simply need to trust him. Like my beautiful niece, we will all get tested. Sometimes we will fall short, sometimes we will fall way short, and other times we will get very close to our goals. And then, one day, we will get a victory. We will win big, and we will know who provided the pathway.

Living a life without Christ leads to a life of uncertainty. It leads to striking at the air hoping we will land a punch. Without Christ, we are vulnerable and alone. We are depending on our own abilities and stamina. While this may work for a long time, there will come a day when we need someone greater than ourselves. All the money in the world cannot fix loneliness, greed, jealousy, hatred, fear, uncertainty, or disappointment.

With the Lord, each circumstance whether you win or fail, becomes a lesson, an understanding, a victory in its own way. You aren't alone because he is always with you. You aren't threatened because he is your shield. You aren't going to die because he is your eternal home. You have rest. You have peace. You get to try again. You don't have to figure everything out. You have an advocate.

Every Saturday, my beautiful niece gave the race everything she had. Every Saturday she learned something she didn't know before. Every Saturday she became stronger, educated, and victorious. She learned where her strength was. She learned how to finish a race. She learned she could be what she was wanting to be. Maybe today needs to be your Saturday. Don't look at what you haven't done. Look at where you are headed. Trust Jesus.

And then, the most important Saturday arrived. The Saturday she had been looking forward to her entire year. The Saturday at the state meet in Austin, Texas. She wasn't about to get caught napping. She wasn't going to get boxed in with the other girls. She came to win, and win was exactly what those beautiful girls did. There is nothing like watching a race. Watching girls you love do their very best for one another. Simple, young girls who came together for a purpose. Young girls who are now champions. One this day, they are the best in the state. One this day, they hold a new school record. There was no missing out today. They all ran for the finish line. She ran her sixty second quarter. They all celebrated a sweetness they had never known.

You are a champion, and you need to see yourself as one. There is a God who gave everything to call you his own. He loves you beyond measure. You have a keen spirit if you will allow him to develop your spiritual acuity. Do you want to train with him?

Try It:

1. Train hard for your goals
2. Believe you are a champion
3. Trust the Holy Spirit to teach you

Scripture: All this I have spoken while still with you. But the Advocate, the Holy Spirit, who the Father will send in my name, will teach you all things and will remind you of everything I have said to you. Peace I leave with you; my peace I give you. I do not give to you as the world gives. Do not let your hearts be troubled and do not be afraid. John 14:25-27

9

"We accept the love we think we deserve."
—Stephen Chbosky[17]

The Washing

Whose Problems Are You Willing to Wash Away?

Focus: Our lives should be so servant-minded that others have a hard time describing the humbleness of our hearts.

Scripture: So, if I, the Master and Teacher, washed your feet, you must now wash each other's feet. I've laid down a pattern for you. What I've done, you do." John 13:14-15

Only once in your life, I truly believe, you find someone who can completely turn your world around. You tell them things that you've never shared with another soul, and they absorb everything you say and actually want to hear more. You share hopes for the future, dreams that will never come true, goals that were never achieved and the many disappointments life has thrown at you.

When something wonderful happens, you can't wait to tell them about it, knowing they will share in your excitement. They are not embarrassed to cry with you when you are hurting or laugh with you when you make a fool of yourself. Never do they hurt your feelings or make you feel like you are not good enough, but rather they build you up and show you the things about yourself that make you special and even beautiful. There is never any pressure, jealousy or competition but only a quiet calmness when they are around. You can be yourself and not worry about what they will think of you because they love you for who you are. The things that seem insignificant to most people such as a note, song or walk become invaluable treasures kept safe in your heart to cherish forever. Memories of your childhood come back and are so clear and vivid it's like being young again. Colors seem brighter and more brilliant. Laughter seems part of daily life where before it was infrequent or didn't exist at all. A phone call or two during the day helps to get you through a long day's work and always brings a smile to your face. In their presence, there's no need for continuous conversation, but you find you're quite content in just having them nearby. Things that never interested you before become fascinating because you know they are important to this person who is so special to you. You think of this person on every occasion and in everything you do. Simple things bring them to mind like a pale blue sky, gentle wind or even a storm cloud on the horizon. You open your heart knowing that there's a chance it may be broken one day and in opening your heart, you experience a love and joy that you never dreamed possible. You find that being vulnerable is the only way to allow your heart to feel true pleasure that's so real it scares you. You find strength in knowing you have a true friend and possibly a soul mate who will remain loyal to the end. Life seems completely different, exciting and worthwhile. Your only hope and security is in knowing that they are a part of your life. —Bob Marley[18]

In the summer of 1989, I was eighteen years old, broke, and in desperate need of a job. A new Burger King was opening in my hometown of Levelland, Texas. I graduated in May, and now it was time to become an adult. Two months later, my future husband would walk through the doors.

I was a former athlete, stout, and competitive. Mitchell, my future husband, was tall, dark-haired, and skinny. He had a great personality and made me laugh. He also aggravated the crud out of me. I have often said I liked him in the morning and hated him in the afternoon. I was gullible, and he was crafty. Let's just say he got the best of me daily.

It's funny how aggravation can grow into fondness. At the time of our meeting, he had a girlfriend, so I figured I shouldn't get too close to him. Our friendship grew, and one day I thought, "he's cute." I made the mistake of telling my friend those words, and the next thing I knew, Mitch and I were eating dinner on our first date. Sitting across from him, I began to realize he was special. One kiss at the door, and I knew: he was the one.

Fast forward thirty-one years to February 2021. My husband's father is sick and close to death. I watch. What do I see? This young man I met in an ugly Burger King uniform now stands like a godly prince as he honors his father. I watch in awe as my husband walks out God's Word every single day. Each decision he is asked to make is more difficult than the day before. Honor is on his lips, actions of love for his father in his steps. I tell my boys regularly, "Watch your father. You can see Jesus through him." Not a day goes by that Mitchell doesn't pray and seek the Lord for his dad.

I have watched Mitch go through tough situations before. I have caused his heart to hurt. I know the pain he faced at the passing of his mom and mine too. But this time, taking care of his dad was different. I wish I could describe what he was like, but my words cannot possibly define his actions. He was directed completely by the Holy Spirit.

His father passed away on February 17, 2021, peacefully. Mitchell stayed the course and moved forward, planning arrangements with his brother, Gary, and making sure Mickey's wishes were carried out. Our hearts melted together, and our love became stronger. God in me, God in us, was now our relationship. Peace that passes all understanding was reality.

"My peace I leave with you." Jesus stated, John 14:27. Jesus, what a beautiful name for such a beautiful person. The true prince gave his life so I might love a man so completely and with such adoration. If not for my Savior, this life would be null. I am reminded of a story in Scripture, a story before death, a story of complete servanthood, a story, until now, was something I wasn't sure I understood, a story of love to the very end. The Washing: John 13

Verses one and two: "Just before the Passover Feast, Jesus knew the time had come to leave this world and go to the Father. Having loved his dear companions, he continued to love them right to the end" (emphasis added).

Right to the end.

Having loved his dear companions, he loved them to the very end. Jesus came so we could see the Father and understand his great love for us. Jesus came in human form, and one of our greatest needs as humans is interaction with other humans. Jesus chose a group to travel with him, talk with him, laugh with him, and grieve with him. He showed them the new, real way to live. They helped him complete his assignment. Although Jesus was God, he chose to become human and live with the same emotions, needs, desires, and frustrations. Jesus needed friends and family. We all need friends and family.

In retrospect, keep in mind that Satan, the god of this world, comes for three things: to kill, steal, and destroy. He comes to kill anything and everyone you love, steal anything and everyone you love, and destroy anything and everyone you love. Jesus knew his time was short. He knew his friends would face fear and hardships. He knew. So, he acted on their behalf and taught them what love looks like.

Before we move forward in Scripture, let's consider human interactions in 2022. Today it seems people are interested in limited communication and one form of communication: small, quick, short, and nonverbal. College students have online options, very few people call each other, churches have video pastors, kids will say hateful things on social media, and we only see everyone's glory days on Facebook. Why? Why have we become so antisocial or false in appearance? What is the root of isolation? Why has Satan worked overtime to put us behind masks?

Why does he want you to not interact with others? Why does he want you afraid and alone? You are much easier to defeat by yourself. The word *isolate(v)* means to detach, to place someone by himself.[10] What arrives by being isolated, left alone, or rejected? What do humans offer? Love, companionship, protections, and unity. The fear of isolation is called autophobia. *Autophobia(s)* can trigger excessive fear, anxiety, avoidance, extreme distress, chronic depression, and an inability to relate to others. [11]

Why would Satan work so hard to keep you isolated? Our own thoughts, if not grounded in Scripture, can cause unreal perception coupled with out-of-control reasoning and questioning. Our minds will create scenarios with unreal answers. People often can't find a way out and begin to contemplate suicidal thoughts.

People need people.

You may think, "People are not trustworthy. I've been hurt too many times." How did Jesus handle betrayal? He included the betrayer. He had dinner with him. He loved him to the very end. John 13:2: *"It was suppertime. The Devil by now had Judas, son of Simon the Iscariot, firmly in his grip, all set for the betrayal."* In black-and-white Scripture, Judas was a friend who ate with Jesus and betrayed him all the same. Yes, people will betray us. Yes, there are mean people. But through Christ, we can be sure he will place amazing people in our lives. No human is perfect. No human doesn't hurt someone else. Humanity is full of people in difficult situations. But inside of a relationship with Christ, he provides a way to be at rest even when our life is in a storm. There is time for less communication, but there are few

---

[10] Webster's 1828 American Dictionary of the English Language, Walking Lion Press, West Valley City, UT, 2010.

[11] Webster's 1828 American Dictionary of the English Language, Walking Lion Press, West Valley City, UT, 2010.

times to remove someone from your life. Violence, of course, is a different matter.

Scripture continues in John 13:3: *"Jesus knew that the Father had put him in complete charge of everything, that he came from God and was on his way back to God. So he got up from the supper table, set aside his robe, and put on an apron."* About four years ago, I went through a devastating tear in my family. A letter was written by a family member that dissolved a relationship with myself, my sisters, and their families. The letter came as a result of a huge confrontation. The letter was a direct arrow to my heart filled with poison, dissatisfaction, unforgiveness, hurt, and blame. It was horrible.

The following year after the letter, I felt I would never have a relationship with this person again. My sisters and I were lost for action or response. We were hurt, angry, and surprised. Isolation now lived in our family. In times like this, which are out of your control, your mind can become an enemy. Not knowing how to fix the situation, understanding the why, or reliving an argument over and over is a very scary place. When there isn't a path forward, you have to learn to live in the middle of the mess.

Jesus had a best friend turn him over to be put to death. Let that sink in. This family member cut me from his life, but he wasn't turning me over to be whipped and nailed to a cross. Maybe that has happened to you. Maybe someone you loved killed someone else. Maybe someone killed someone you loved. To be honest, you haven't even been able to recover. Devastation is now a member of your family.

What did Jesus do? Do you think because he was God, he didn't hurt, didn't feel, and didn't become upset? Yes, he did. He felt all of those things. His best friend turned on him. His best friend sold him for silver. Humanity is ugly. John 13:5: "*Then he poured water into a basin and began to wash the feet of the disciples, drying them with his apron. Peter, one of his friends, pleaded with him to not wash his feet. Jesus replied, 'You don't understand now what I'm doing, but it will be clear enough to you later.'*"

Jesus was washing his disciples' feet. He was cleaning the dirt from their travels away. When we accept Christ, he goes to work washing the dirt from our travels away. We don't even understand what he is doing; he just begins to wash away the broken pieces and dries them with his towel. He loves us to the very end. Life brings situations when we need someone to care for us, wash the dirt from us, and love us. And at other times, we need to do that for someone else. I watched my husband wash the feet of his father on more than one occasion.

Peter continued to protest. Jesus replied, "*If I don't wash you, you can't be a part of what I'm doing.*" Being washed by Christ is the only way to redemption. He is the only one who can change us from the inside out. Humanity is ugly. Jesus needed to wash his followers first so we, in turn, can wash others in his name. We can't skip steps. There are amazing people who do big things for others, but they are missing the supernatural side. Jesus fills a void, cleans us up, and puts us back on our feet. No other human can do what he does.

Judas, his friend, had his feet washed too. But Judas acted in ritual, not from a redemptive heart. He wasn't healed or changed. His mindset kept him in bondage. As Jesus finished up, he continued, "*Do you understand what I have done for you? You address me as Teacher or Master, and rightly so. That is what I am. So, if I, the Master, and Teacher, washed your feet, you must now wash each other's feet. I've laid down a pattern for you. What I've done, you do.*" *John 13: 13-15.* Our job is to accept Jesus and allow him to heal us and wash away the dirt in our lives. We are to show love to those who don't know him. He expects Christians, Christ followers, to love other humans. People get to choose. He laid down a pattern. Whose problems are you willing to wash away?

Jesus finished by stating, "'*Make sure you get this right: Receiving someone I sent is the same as receiving me, just as receiving me is the same as receiving the one who sent me.' After he said these things, Jesus became visibly upset and then he told them why, 'One of you is going to betray me.'*" John 13:20-21. Jesus became visibly upset. One of his friends was going to send him to his death. One of his friends.

In the story with this family member, I became visibly upset. Someone I loved was cutting me out of his life. I learned a lot through that situation, but my greatest victory was understanding how much my heavenly Father wanted me to be happy. In the absence of this person, I found a new relationship with my spiritual Father. We all have a choice. We all have a Bible. God loves us. But it will always be our choice. Over time, the Lord worked through me to reach out to this person. He was hurt, I was hurt, and my sisters were hurt, but washing feet became a priority. The Holy Spirit guided my feet to step out, and he cleaned them when the dirt (problems) clouded them.

I kept moving forward. Mitch kept moving forward. When the Lord gives you a task, a responsibility, a calling, he washes your feet along the way. He knows ahead of time what you will face. But he loves others too. He may send you where you'll get dirty, but at night, he will wash the dirt from your feet, settle your heart and mind, and give you rest. If he sets a pattern for us to follow, then he will do what we cannot, strengthen us when we are tired, and wash our weary feet. Even if our own troubles are great, we would find a way to serve.

Will every situation change? Maybe not. Judas left at night with a piece of bread from Jesus's table. But that is a discussion for another time.

Try It:

1. Ask the Lord to wash your feet.
2. Ask the Lord for a person to wash his/her feet.
3. Forgive.

Scripture: "Do you understand what I have done for you? You address me as Teacher or Master, and rightly so. That is what I am. So if I, the Master and Teacher, washed your feet, you must now wash each other's feet. I've laid down a pattern for you. What I've done, you do." —John 13:13-15.

10

"One's best success comes after their greatest disappointments." —Henry Ward Beecher[19]

Don't Be Afraid of "No"

How Do We Handle Disappointment?

Focus: Allow God to be the strongest when you are at your weakest.

Scripture: "Moses objected, 'They won't trust me. They won't listen to a word I say. They're going to say, God? Appeared to him? Hardly!'" Exodus 4:11

When I was little, one of my favorite cartoons was *Peanuts*. Snoopy is still a favorite today. Throughout all the episodes, there is one scene that is reoccurring: Lucy and the football. The audience watches as Charlie Brown wonders if Lucy can be trusted. If you've never seen what happens, it goes something like this. Lucy tempts Charlie Brown to kick a football while she holds it in place. She promises to hold the ball steady and straight so he can run hard and fast to kick the ball.

Unfortunately, time and time again, she yanks the ball away from him at the last second, and he falls on his back. She continues to promise not to do it. Charlie Brown always recalls his previous kick and doubts her reliability. Yet, somehow, repeatedly, she manages to get him to trust her. Not one time does she hold the ball steady; not one time does Charlie Brown get to kick the ball.[20] What makes him hope against all odds that this time will be different? Why does he continue to trust an untrustworthy person? Why does he expect different results by continuing to place his trust in an unreliable source?

The accuser is an unreliable source. He is the master at getting us to believe things will be just fine if we trust him. He is good at promising false results, especially for people vulnerable to the need for acceptance or love. The accuser also knows what is the most valuable in your life, and he wants to make you believe he is the answer to those concerns. In Luke 4:5–8, the Bible gives us an example of how the accuser tried to tempt Jesus with the same approach. He used what was most important to Jesus, you and me. Luke 4:5-8:

> *Then the Devil took him up and revealed to him all the kingdoms of the world in a moment of time. The Devil told him, "I will give you the glory of these kingdoms and authority over them-because they are mine to give to anyone I please. I will give it all to you if you will bow down and worship me." Jesus replied, "The Scriptures say, 'You must worship the Lord your God; serve him only.'"*

Satan, the accuser, was tempting Jesus to bow before him in order to save the kingdoms of the world. The kingdoms of the world are you and me, mankind. Satan was letting Jesus know he was in control and that the only way to save these pitiful humans was for Satan to give him authority. Satan wanted Jesus to recognize who he was and bow before his stolen kingship. Satan doesn't own anything; he is a fake. He only has authority when we give it to him. Jesus didn't argue with him and tell him he was the Son of God. He didn't belittle him or use his power on him. He quoted Scripture to him. He used his Father's Word to defeat Satan. There is a lesson in this if we take the time to study it.

God's Word was the beginning of all creation. God's Word is the word all creation bows to. Jesus knew his Father, our Father, is the creator. God is not a fake. God is the great I AM. Jesus is teaching us that no matter what the situation is presented by the accuser, the answer is the Word of God. If we can really get that understanding down deep in our hearts, then understanding the Bible becomes our priority, and receiving its power and authority becomes our focus. Adjusting my thoughts to the reality of Scripture is an everyday battle. It is worth the fight.

There are times in my life when I felt like Charlie Brown. I have placed my trust in someone I thought was trustworthy only to learn he, she, or it was not. There have also been times I put my trust in Scripture, but the result I was hoping for didn't come. Now what? This is the place of careful footing. I believe this is a rock face, a place where a giant fall is certain if we don't guard our hearts and read the Bible. When we stand on promises that are not fulfilled in our minds, we must run to Jesus and hide in his love, or the accuser will purposely yank us right off the mountain. He will move the football, and onto our backs we will fall.

Satan roams about looking for this opportunity. He waits, and he loves to say, "God doesn't love you. God let this happen.

Where is God now?" Yes, he accuses you in the courts of heaven, and he accuses God in your mind. He is the expert divider.

It is when we are the most disappointed or battle weary that Satan comes to devour what is left of us. He has worked diligently to get us to this place in our lives. He is patient and happy to wait for our disappointment. In a previous chapter, I wrote about a little girl with leukemia. I wrote about her because she and her entire family are precious to me. Through this little baby's journey, she changed lives. She opened eyes and gave people hope. I would love to say that she is walking the earth today, but that isn't what happened.

"I've never met a strong person with an easy past." —Zig Ziglar[21]

In the middle of this fight, I was given a clear vision that leukemia had left her body. She literally spit it out. When she went to be with Jesus, I was confused. I wondered if what I saw was real. I began to question in areas I really didn't want to question. What do you do when you've done all you know to do and the answer doesn't come? I buried myself deep in the Word like a blanket. I listened to Bill Johnson. I prayed. This is what I learned.

There are mysteries in life. There are times when our human reasons cannot answer questions that are beyond our understanding. We have to say, "I don't understand, but I trust the Lord." If we will trust God in our brokenness, he will mend us in a way only he can. We can't make up solutions in our mind just to give ourselves closure. Death is a part of life. We will all die. We just leave this earth at different times.

God understands grief, tears, and anguish. He holds all of our tears deep in his heart and wants to help us. He never tries to hurt us. So how do we get better after trauma? We sing, rest, pray, and say, "God, what do you want me to learn from this?"

Not so you can point blame, but so you can be at peace and stronger in the future.

The disciples were in a similar situation in Matthew 17. The disciples were the "group" back in the time of Jesus. They followed him around with non-stop access. They learned from him daily. Jesus hand-selected them and gave them power. The disciples were smart, young, and eager. Matthew 17:14–16 describes a time when the disciples prayed and failed.

When they arrived at the foot of the mountain, a huge crowd was waiting for them. A man came and knelt before Jesus and said, "Lord have mercy on my son, because he has seizures and suffers terribly. He often falls into the fire or in the water. So I brought him to your disciples, but they couldn't heal him."

If anyone should have been able to help this man and his son, it would have been the disciples. I am sure they did everything they had seen Jesus do. They used their authority and the correct words, yet nothing happened. The disciples failed. The men who walked with Jesus every day failed. They encountered a situation they didn't know how to defeat. If this happens to them, it will happen to us.

When this occurred, I found Jesus's reply a little hard to accept. He didn't comfort the disciples; he challenged them to do better. Matthew 17: 17-18: "*Jesus responded, 'You stubborn, faithless people. How long must I be with you until you believe? How long must I put up with you? Bring the boy to me.' Then Jesus rebuked the demon in the boy, and it left him. From that moment the boy was well.*" We might think Jesus was a bit hard on the disciples, but every single one of them wanted to know what happened. Failure wasn't an option. They knew they needed further understanding. They didn't give up and run the other way. They didn't go sit in a pit. They stood up and realized Jesus was the answer, and they needed to learn from him.

Matthew 17:19
Afterward, the disciples asked Jesus privately, "Why couldn't we cast out that demon?" Jesus answered, "You didn't have enough faith. I assure you, even if you had faith as small as a mustard seed you could say to this mountain, move from here to there, and it would move. Nothing would be impossible."

Jesus is saying to believe and not doubt. Create a faith base in your life that doesn't seem impossible. This is easier said than done. The lesson to learn is, "Help me not to doubt, Lord. If I apply for a job and I don't get it, help me not to doubt. If I pray for someone, and his miracle doesn't come, help me not to doubt. Help me, Lord, to not doubt in the beginning and reason in the end." It's hard!

In Mark 9:17–29, the same story appears but with a little more detail. Let's go back to where Jesus was speaking to the father about his son and review more of the conversation between the two. Mark 9:20-21:

So they brought the boy. But when the evil spirit saw Jesus, it threw the child into a violent convulsion, and he fell to the ground, writhing and foaming at the mouth. "How long has this been happening?" Jesus asked the boy's father. He replied, "Since he was very small. The evil spirit often

makes him fall into the fire or into water, trying to kill him.
Have mercy on us and help us. Do something if you can."

The man's reply was either a statement or a question. Either way, it was a big response to the Son of God. However, I admire him for speaking what he was thinking. He had seen many people, including Jesus's disciples, try to remove this spirit from his son, and all had failed. I am sure he was hopeful, but doubtful. This thought is still running around today. For example, if someone we love has fought a long battle with cancer, do we really believe they can be healed? Or do we just hope, with little belief it will really happen?

Mark 9:23: *"'What do you mean, "If I can'?'" Jesus asked.* *'Anything is possible if a person believes.'"* This is where I often stop and say, "Yes, but this is Christ, the Son of God, the Messiah. How on earth am I supposed to have a faith like his? I don't know. All I do know is Jesus gave me the Holy Spirit. Jesus gave me his peace. Jesus gave me his authority. So, somehow, I must learn to trust the Holy Spirit completely. I don't even think I have to memorize Scripture or even know how to pray. I just need to learn to use the Word. I need to train my mind to respond to everything with the Word of God. Is it okay to be honest with the Lord and say, "Help me, Lord. Help me believe in you. Help me with my unbelief." Let's take a look at how the man responded to what Jesus answered.

Mark 9:24: *"The father instantly replied, 'I do believe, but help me not to doubt!'"* Thank you, Lord, for this verse; it helps me. Thank you for showing me that we are weak. Thank you for showing me I need you to help me with doubt. The man is saying, "Yes, I believe in who you are. My trouble is in believing you will help me." I don't think this man had any doubt Jesus was the Son of God. I don't think he worried about Jesus's power. I think he wondered whether he was worthy of asking for his help. I am sure he asked himself, "Why would God help me?" I think this is one of the biggest lies of the accuser. It isn't that we struggle in believing God is the creator and can do all things but accepting the enormous amount of love he has for us. More than understanding who hates you, you need to understand who loves you. You need to have the same ideas as Jesus.

God isn't surprised by our lack of faith. It is in our times of weakness that he becomes the strongest. There are times when the Lord will purposely send us into a battle where he knows the answer is no. At times, the Lord will send us over and over into the same situation, and the answer doesn't come. For example, you pray for a person you love to get saved, change their perspective, or forgive. The situation seems to be getting worse. Their attitude changes, and it becomes nasty. They may withdraw or not talk to you. Why does this happen? People learn to harden their hearts. Yet, God continues to send you, knowing you will be rejected, knowing you will hear a "no." Why? Someone has to go and be his voice. Hard hearts don't frighten God. In fact, the harder the heart, the bigger the reward when it softens. What does God see in humanity to continue to send someone into a fight he or she isn't winning? The cause is greater than the sacrifice.

Why does God make us ask for help from people he knows will reject us? Keep in mind that their answers are not a surprise to him. He can see their hearts. He knows how they will respond before we ever approach them. Therefore, when rejection is staring us in our face, we must remember our whole life has already been planned by God. He knows every outcome. He has placed us in this time for a predestined purpose.

This is evident in the story of Moses.

Moses was sent by the Lord to Pharaoh, the king of Egypt, to ask him to let the people of Israel, who were slaves of Egypt, to be released from captivity. God sent Moses to release the people so they could go and worship Him. Moses was sent ten times to Pharaoh with the same request, each time getting the same answer, "no." Moses was purposely sent to ask Pharaoh to let God's people go. God knew Pharaoh's heart, and he knew he would say no before Moses ever approached him. Yet the Lord continued to send him. Just because we expect a certain answer does not mean we will get it. God sees what we cannot see. This is why Jesus continues to preach to us about our faith and trusting God no matter what the result is.

God understands our frustration and unwillingness to continue in a battle we are losing. Consider the conversation Moses had with God on more than one occasion. In Exodus 3:7–8, God had decided to rescue his people from Egypt. He told Moses the people had suffered long enough, and he would go to pry them from the hands of Pharaoh. However, he needed a man to be his mouthpiece. The man selected was Moses. Moses, on the other hand, wasn't really excited about the selection. He replied in verse 11: "'*But why me? What makes you think I could ever go to Pharaoh and lead the children of Israel out of Egypt?' 'I'll be with you,' God said. 'And this will be the proof that I sent you: When you have brought my people out of Egypt, you will worship God right here at this very mountain.*'" The conversation continued, "'*Suppose I go to the people of Israel and I tell them, "The God of your fathers sent me to you:" and they ask me, 'What is his name? What should I tell them?'" God said to Moses, 'I-AM-WHO-I-AM. Tell the people of Israel, "I AM sent me to you."'*"

Moses had been guaranteed by God himself that he had been commissioned to go to the people of Israel and tell them he would lead them out of Egypt at the great I AM's request. He was told by God to do this. In fact, God was speaking to Moses through a burning bush as he gave him this directive. If anyone believed he would have a victory, it would have been Moses. Even though Moses knew he couldn't work this miracle on his own, he had been drafted by God himself and given a direct order. I am sure Moses was still a bit nervous, but God told him to gather some leadership around him and get moving.

As Moses set out to free the children of Israel, focusing on God's love and walking in obedience to Egypt, God knew Pharaoh had no intention of letting the people go. God knew Pharaoh had a hard heart, had no reverence for him, and would not grant freedom for any child of the Most High. God knew, yet he still sent Moses to ask. God wasn't surprised by Pharaoh's answer.

If God knew these answers when he sent Moses, he knows answers before he sends us. As I have studied Exodus, God is teaching me this is the trust and faith he is asking us to develop. I think sometimes when we pray, we believe the result we are asking for is the best result. God asks us to come boldly to the throne and make our requests known to him, to believe what we ask for and continue to ask for it. He commissions us to be bold warriors with childlike faith and ask our Father in heaven to grant our requests. He wants to see us begin our walk, like Moses and conquer our giant in front of us. But sometimes he doesn't answer the first time. Sometimes others are involved, their wills must be subjected to God's will, and, at times, this may take years.

The lesson I have learned is to pray like a champion. Fight for what I want to see happen. Don't give in. But understand that I can't see everything God sees. I can't investigate another's heart, and I can't make people do what is right. Therefore, when things do not work out the first time, I need to remember that the Lord is still in control and does listen to my prayers. He hears my cries for help and is moving on my behalf. It just may take longer than I expect it to. God may be using me like Moses. Will I have the strength to continue down a path where I am getting beat up to save people? Will I stay in the fight and continue to ask a source that has no love for anything? How many "no's" am I willing to endure to get the result I am expecting? How long am I willing to wait?

God isn't surprised by the "no" of this world. He never gives up. He continues to work on my behalf because he loves me. If I am willing to trust God's love for me, I have this promise, *"All things work together for those who love the Lord and are called according to his word"* (Romans. 8:28). A negative answer doesn't stop my Father in heaven. It doesn't scare him. He doesn't give up. He loves me too much to watch me suffer. He is working on my behalf. I just need to trust him in all things.

As the story continues, Moses continues to talk with the Lord and raise concerns. He isn't just worried about Pharaoh's authority but how the people of Israel will react to him. In Exodus 4:1, *"Moses objected, 'They won't trust me. They won't listen to a word I say. They're going to say, God? Appeared to him? Hardly!'"* God gave Moses several signs he could perform to demonstrate the power of God that worked through him. The Lord equipped Moses to be able to convince people he had been sent from God. The Lord will equip us to demonstrate his power to help people believe.

Moses continued to complain to the Lord. Exodus 4:10: "*Moses raised another objection to God: 'Master, please, I don't talk well, I've never been good with words, neither before nor after you spoke to me. I stutter and stammer.'*" 4:11: "*God said, 'And who do you think made the human mouth? And who makes some mute, gives him sight or makes him blind? Now go! I will help you speak, and I will teach you what to say.'*" The Lord will help me speak and teach me what to say. As long as he is first in my life, and I am praying for his will over my life, the Lord will be my words. He will give the words to say. The words I speak have power.

As we read through these conversations, the Lord was equipping Moses through works of his hands and mouth. The frailties Moses saw in himself were addressed by God. God wasn't sending Moses into battle without first spending time with him, strengthening him, and encouraging him. God was making sure that Moses understood he wasn't walking alone. However, he continued to push him along. He told him to get going and move on. He didn't let him sit around and worry. He wanted him to continue to move forward even though he knew when Moses made his first request to Pharaoh, the answer would be no, and the people of Israel would not be happy with Moses. The future would get worse before it gets better. Pharaoh had no intention to let his slave labor go free. In fact, he would become very angry, and the people of Israel would suffer for it.

I AM sent Moses. Moses's future was not a surprise to God. Over and over the course of the next chapters in Exodus, Moses was sent to Pharaoh with the same request: let the people of Israel go so they could worship the Lord. The request never changed. God's mind never changed. Pharaoh's heart hardened. Pharaoh's heart said no. Pharaoh's heart was the issue.

Situations today are no different than the situation Moses was facing. People today are still slaves. Maybe not to a Pharaoh, but they are slaves. They are slaves to anger, bitterness, poverty, addiction, or hatred. They are slaves to their bank accounts or their secret lives. They are slaves to secrets. Some are imprisoned by it; others are just miserable. The choices of yesterday have determined their present. People are praying for them. A modern-day Moses or helper is sent to do the work. What Moses or helper needs to understand is that the answer of rejection is high. "No" is probably going to be the first answer.

Maybe a family has been split apart because of death, misunderstanding, or new people. There is a curse of bitterness and selfishness that was placed on the family by grandparents. Bitterness and pity have rooted in two of the members. They do not like one another and blame each other for mistreatment and disrespect. It tears the family apart. God chooses a helper to try and build a road between the two. The one selected to be obedient to God finds herself in a position that is much like Moses. She doesn't want to be the mouthpiece. She doesn't want to be the one in the middle. It causes more problems and fewer solutions. She is in danger of losing both relationships, and she considers which one is more important to her. How does she determine what to do?

Through understanding Moses's story, she begins to realize God sees the hearts of the two she loves. She also realizes she can't change how they feel about each other. She will continue to be the mouthpiece as God shows her what to say. God's love for all of them hasn't changed. His desire for them to be a family again hasn't changed. He wants to heal all of their hearts. God isn't going to quit, give up, or change his mind. He loves all of them, and he will have a victory. The longer it takes to get them to see the light, the bigger the reward in the end. As the Moses of this family continues to spend time with God, her prayers of reconciliation don't change. God will come through. God will deliver her family out of the bonds of unforgiveness.

God is a reliable source. He isn't going to make us run toward the football and move it like Lucy. He doesn't purposely hurt us. He is teaching us that we must trust him above all else. He may send us into a battle we will lose for a while. We may be rejected. We may not get the answer we hoped for. But God's will won't change. His thoughts for our lives don't change. He isn't scared. We must stay active in studying God's Word. We must continue to pray and ask questions. We need to trust him with our fears and with those we love more than anything. Someone has to kick the football.

Try It:

1. Don't be afraid of "No"!
2. Choose to be a Moses.
3. Learn to continue in what the Lord calls you to do.

Scripture: "Moses objected. 'They won't trust me. They won't listen to a word I say. They are going to say, God? Appeared to him? Hardly!'" Exodus 4:11

11

"I don't run to add days to my life, I run to add life to my days." —Ronald Roark[22]

Keep the Dog Behind the Fence

Who Will You Listen To?

Focus: I am a contender.

Scripture: "I train like a champion athlete running my race to win a victor's crown that will last forever" (1 Cor. 9:25).

It is 6:00 a.m. I wake up and eat my oatmeal and drink coffee in a regular cup. I watch Joyce Meyer on TV. It's summertime, the air is cool, and the sun is bright. It is time for a run, so I change into my gear: shorts, sports bra, running shoes, and a tank top. Headphones are charged, and Spotify is on my phone. My hair is pulled back, and I am ready for three miles with the Lord. It is time to spend forty-five minutes with my best friend, Jesus. This is truly what I love the most: sunshine, music, and time with the Lord.

The time I completely hand over to the Lord is when I am running or walking. I just want to spend time with him. It is a treasured time. I am simply myself. I don't need to be anyone else. *"For that reason, I don't run just for exercise or box like one throwing aimless punches, but I train like a champion athlete. I subdue my body and get in under my control, so that after preaching the good news to others I won't be disqualified"* (1 Cor. 9:26). I long for these times.

Often, God will use nature to teach me. In fact, He has given me visions of angels in the trees. He has taught me about life through rivers and has provided clarity by watching birds. I have learned prosperity lessons through pine and oak trees. I have laughed plenty by watching the squirrels in our yard. God is present everywhere. We just need to look for him and let him show up. He is our creator.

I head out the door ready to have fun. I invite Jesus to join me, "Let's go, Jesus." In my mind, I am about five years old again. I am running and giggling with my best friend. I imagine we are holding hands, and he is smiling at me. My big brother, Jesus, is with me, and I can't wait for what he will show me. It is fun, and I am excited. The first song comes on. I know every word. I praise the Lord. I sing as loud as I can. I don't care who hears me. I just sing and sing, letting God know how grateful I am to be his daughter. I keep time with the music, pretending I'm running my race, singing to the Lord, and finishing like a champion. I hold my hands up high in praise. I am happy to be alive and thankful I can run.

As I complete the next few miles, new songs come along, and my pace gets slower, then faster. The Lord and I just talk back and forth. I ask questions, and he listens.

On my journey, I ran by several fences. Many of these fences have what I call yippy dogs in the backyards. As I run along, I can hear them barking at me. I can tell I am aggravating them. They bark, growl, and fuss at me as I run by. Every now and then, one of them will startle me. Today my father says, "You know the accuser is a lot like those dogs. He comes at you like a barking dog through the spirit of fear. He wants you to stop or reroute just because you hear a bark or a growl." As Christians, the closer we get to our breakthrough, the closer we get to our victory, the louder the accuser barks. God simply said, "Keep the dog behind the fence and keep running."

The accuser cannot get to us behind the fence of God's protection. We are not to allow the dog or the spirit of fear to distract, frighten, or detour us in any way. The reality is that you will run right by the problem. Keep running and focusing on the love of God. Keep moving and see your finish line. Turn up the music and allow the Holy Spirit to set the pace for your run of life. Keep the dog behind the fence. *"But the Lord Yahweh is always faithful to place you on a firm foundation and guard you from the Evil One"* (2 Thess. 3:3).

Fear is a liar! He comes just like a barking dog. He will whisper lies, such as, "You'll never make it." "You're going to die from this disease." "I am taking your child." "Your husband won't survive." "No one loves you." "You will go bankrupt." "No one will ever forgive you." Fear is the opposite of truth. Fear wars against the reality of Scripture. The job of fear is to take your eyes off Jesus and get your mouth to confess the lies. Satan is a liar. He will stop you on your run. He will bark and not stop. Put fear behind the fence and run right by. Did Jesus face temptation? Absolutely. Let's take a look at how he handled it.

In Matthew 4:1-3: Jesus was to be tempted by the devil. The Passion Translation states:

Afterward, the Holy Spirit led Jesus into the lonely wilderness in order to reveal his strength against the accuser by going through the ordeal of testing. And after fasting for forty days, Jesus was extremely weak and famished. Then the tempter came to entice him to provide food by doing a miracle. So, he said to Jesus, "How can you possibly be the Son of God and go hungry? Just order these stones to be turned into loaves of bread."

Before we study the response of Jesus, let's look at what the accuser was trying to do.

If we look at the context of this passage, we should review what happened just prior to this piece of Scripture. At the end of chapter 3, God had spoken from the sky about who Jesus was. Matthew 3:17 states, *"Then suddenly the voice of the Father shouted from the sky, saying, 'This is the Son I love, and my greatest delight is in him.'"* Stop and think about that.

God had declared who Jesus was and how much he loved him right before the nasty devil came to challenge Jesus. Keep this in perspective as you look at your own life. In Colossians 2:9-10, we find our identity in Jesus, *"For he is the complete fullness of deity living in human form. And our own completeness is now found in him."* When we accept Jesus into our lives as Lord and Savior, God says, "This is my child; you belong to me, and all of my promises are for you. I will never leave or forsake you." Immediately what does Satan do? He comes to take all of that from you. He wants you to doubt your identity. He tries to tempt all of us into thinking the opposite of what God says.

We must condition our minds to know and believe Scripture in all situations. Yes, condition your mind. It is a choice to believe what we believe. You must be a contender for what you believe and expect to see.

As we continue to look at this Scripture, let us not forget who went with Jesus in his temptation. *"Afterward the Holy Spirit led Jesus into the lonely wilderness."* The Holy Spirit went with him. The Holy Spirit goes with us and marches right beside us. He doesn't leave us. He doesn't just watch and let us suffer alone. He comforts us and gives us Scripture. He stands us up when we get knocked down and stays with us. He doesn't give up. He stands in the hospital room when a diagnosis comes back. He sits in the room full of bitterness between family members. How we respond in situations like these determines the amount of authority we give him to move on our behalf.

Next, the Bible says for Jesus to reveal his strength, he was tested. Verse 1 continues, *"In order to reveal his strength against the accuser by going through the ordeal of testing."* The word *ordeal(s)* means a painful or horrific experience.[12] An ordeal is like trauma. Jesus allowed himself to be subject to a primitive means of determining guilt or innocence by submitting himself to dangerous or painful tests believed to be under supernatural control. Why would God allow Jesus to undergo dangerous or painful tests? Jesus was to show his strength and determine his reliance on God. He was defining his identity.

In order for Jesus to reveal his strength, he was tested. You mean a test is to show my strength? A test should reveal what I know? A test should be the time to tell the accuser he messed

---

[12] Webster's 1828 American Dictionary of the English Language, Walking Lion Press, West Valley City, UT, 2010.

with the wrong person. But I don't feel that way. Let's take a look at another piece of Scripture to encourage ourselves when we don't "feel" capable of passing the test. 1 Corinthians 10:13: *We all experience times of testing, which is normal for every human being. But God will be faithful to you. He will screen and filter the severity, nature, and timing of every test or trial you face so that you can bear it. And each test is an opportunity to trust him more, for along with every trial God has provided for you a way of escape that will bring you out of it victoriously."*

Each test is an opportunity to trust him more. How? Jesus was tempted because he wanted to prove to you and me that we can face anything or anyone. He wanted to be the example of what to do when you are tested. You are not defeated; you are tested. If you allow the Holy Spirit to guide you in the test, then you will pass the test. Your strength in trusting God will be the victory. Are you going to listen to the dog or run right on by?

As we continue with this Scripture, we see that Jesus was extremely weak and famished. In verse 2, it says, *"And after fasting for forty days, Jesus was extremely weak and famished."* I don't know of very many people who have fasted for forty days. I have a hard time not drinking coffee in the morning. I cannot imagine the self-discipline it takes to fast for forty days. We can all relate to being hungry and tired. Satan came directly at him regarding food. Jesus was hungry. Jesus was the Son of God. So, the accuser went directly at his human basic needs. The accuser asked, *"How can you possibly be the Son of God and go hungry? Just order these stones to be turned into loaves of bread."*

How many times does Satan come for your basic human need? He always strikes our needs. He always comes after our health or finances. But according to Philippians 4:19, *"My God will supply all my needs according to His glorious riches in Christ*

Jesus." Jesus was defending this Scripture when he responded to the devil. He knew what was at hand when he was tested. He stopped the accuser in his tracks so that Philippians 4:19 could become real for us. Our Jesus is the Champion. He had a Champion's response.

Matthew 4:4 continues, "*He answered, 'The Scriptures say: Bread alone will not satisfy, but true life is found in every word, which constantly goes forth from God's mouth.'*" Food does not satisfy; the steadfast Word of God does. The Word is steadfast and constant. God's Word does not change. What shall we choose to eat? Shall we choose to eat the bread that comes from God's mouth, his Word? Or shall we choose to eat the lies of the accuser? Shall we believe what is staring us in the eye? Shall we listen to the dog bark? Shall we let him out of the fence? Or maybe we should believe the Bible, put our faith in Jesus, and keep on running. Jesus's strength came by understanding his identity and answering the accuser with God's Word.

As believers in Christ, we must:

- Know who we are in Christ
- Recognize the Bible as our weapon of truth
- Use the word as our sword in a test
- Rest in the peace of allowing God's Word to resolve the situation
- Give thanks

Understanding our identity in Christ brings heaven to earth. This was not the last time Jesus was tempted. Continue to read Matthew 4 for revelation on how Jesus continued to answer the devil each time he tried to test him. When Jesus was finished with the tests, he told the accuser to go away. Once Jesus revealed his strength in God, Satan left, and angels gathered around and ministered to Jesus. The very same thing happens to us. Angels gather around us and minister to us daily. The more God's strength is demonstrated through us, the more tests we will pass.

I believe the Lord gave me the example of the dog because in our protection from the Father, Satan is contained. He is confined and is only let loose when someone opens the gate. We open or close the gate through words we speak. Life and death are in the power of the tongue. If I don't stop to let the dog out, then he is confined to his space. He has no authority in my life. Until I release him, he cannot hurt me. The minute we allow words to blast from our mouths that war against Scripture, the accuser is allowed to attack.

Recently a dear friend of mine helped me to see how a dog's bark can be very frightening. About two weeks before Christmas break, a friend of mine came to my classroom during my conference time. We began talking, and I asked her how her husband was. John is a mighty man of God who recently won the battle against cancer. Immediately when I asked her about John, she began to cry. She said that she didn't know why she was telling me this; she hadn't even told her family. Through shoulder surgery, the doctors found a spot on John's lung. He was scheduled for an MRI on Friday. She looked at me and said, "I am so scared."

I began to pray in the spirit as she talked. I listened. She understood how God was bigger than this finding, but she was scared all the same. I totally understood how fear could be a giant in the room. When she finished talking, I simply asked, "Did God take care of John the first time?" "Yes," she replied. "And isn't he faithful enough to do it again?" I asked. "Yes," she said, shaking. "Okay then, let's put the dog behind the fence and speak God's Word into this situation." She looked at me kind of strangely. I began to tell her the story. She laughed and said, "I know better. I haven't been speaking God's Word into this situation. I have allowed the barking dog of fear to scare the daylights out of me." I told her I could understand perfectly as to why she would react that way. We are certainly not perfect, and God understands that. I told her that I also believed the Lord sent her to me because she needed a friend to help strengthen her mind and her confession.

We prayed in my classroom and asked the Lord for complete and total healing. We agreed this spot would be absolutely nothing and for God to be glorified in this victory. The MRI would be in two days. We hugged and believed in God for the best.

On Friday, I was home when my phone rang. It was a text from my friend. She said, "The MRI was negative. John is just fine. I sure am glad we kept the dog behind the fence." I cried and shouted and gave praise to my Lord. That day was a banner day for my friend. It was a day to stand on when other clouds came her way. It was a victory for me as well. I felt like a champion. I ran my race, and God ran with me.

Let's take a look at some common fears and base our response from Scripture. Jesus is our example. He responded to every temptation with the Word of God. It is time to have our sword of the spirit ready. It is time to have the right response.

Fear Of: Not having financial needs met
Truth Is: The Lord has you covered in every area of life.
Scripture: Philippians 4:19: "My God shall supply all of my needs according to his riches and glory in Jesus Christ."

Fear Of: Failing
Truth Is: We don't fail; we just learn and get back up.
Scripture: Philippians 4:19: "I can do all things through Christ who strengthens me."

Fear Of: Sickness and disease
Truth Is: Sickness and disease are illegal to our bodies.
Scripture: Isaiah 53:5: "But he was wounded for our transgressions, he was bruised for our iniquities: the chastisement of our peace was upon him; and with his stripes we were healed."

Fear Of: Worry and anxiety
Truth Is: I have a sound mind.
Scripture: 2 Timothy 1:7: "For God will never give you the spirit of fear, but the Holy Spirit who gives you mighty power, love, and self-control (sound mind)."

Fear Of: Loneliness
Truth Is: He is always with you wherever your feet travel.
Scripture: Deuteronomy 31:8: "It is the Lord who goes before you. He will be with you; he will not leave you or forsake you. Do not fear or be dismayed."

Try It:

1. Go for a walk.
2. Chew on Scripture.
3. Keep the dog behind the fence.

Scripture: "I train like a champion athlete running my race to win a victor's crown that will last forever" (1 Cor. 9:25). I am a contender.

12

"God's love is so extravagant and so inexplicable that he loved us before we were us."
— *Judah Smith, Head Pastor of Churchhome.*[23]

Ruined for Normal

What Do You Know about Mysteries?

Focus: A new standard of glory will rest in your life.

Mark 4:11: "The privilege of intimately knowing the mystery of God's kingdom realm has been given to you" (TPT).

Quoted from Brian Simmons, author of the Passion Translation:

You will speak a message of truth and grace with your life. You will walk in a new level of my power and anointing. You will begin to live as your Father in heaven-holy, pure, and filled with faith. As you set your heart on me, give your thoughts to me, and surrender your cares to me, a new standard of glory will operate in your life. Everything changes when you become consumed with the reality of my life working in you. My presence makes you act and think differently and even changes your physical appearance. When your heart is yielded to me, you release the fragrance of heaven effortlessly (emphasis added).

In the year 2016, God gave me a desire to study the book of Revelation. Before this time, I had always been intimidated to study the book mainly because of its use of imagery and interpretation of end times. I was concerned that I wouldn't be able to understand it and that I would be left with more questions than answers. What I have learned over the last seven years of deep study of Scripture is that if you ask God for understanding, he will give it to you. He gives answers and piques our curiosity, so we continue to dig, read, and ask. Each mystery provides a segue to the next one. God is a mystery, and little by little, he shows us just how majestic he truly is.

One of the big understandings he gave me during my study of Revelation was an insight on the characteristics of his kingdom found in Revelation 21. I was baffled by the precision of his kingdom, including the size and the jewels. This is an abbreviated version of what the Lord showed me on the importance of the jewels.

The kingdom of God is leveled in the most beautiful gems. Take time to look them up on the internet so you can see them in their purest form. Each level is 216 feet thick. He has them lined up like a rainbow, one nestled up to the next. The levels, starting from bottom to top, are:

1. Bottom layer: Jasper
2. Sapphire
3. Agate

4. Emerald
5. Onyx
6. Carnelian
7. Chrysolite
8. Beryl
9. Topaz
10. Chrysoprase
11. Jacinth
12. Top Layer: Amethyst

Revelation 21:15–27

The stones have their own meaning and characteristics. They are layered for a purpose. The first six are foundational stones, foundational ideas every Christian should understand. The levels of the colors are a progression ladder. Each level is a new understanding of the majesty, power, and character of God. A Christian can pray for revelation knowledge as he or she moves up the ladder.

Let's begin with level one, jasper. Jasper is red in color. It is the foundational stone that represents Jesus's blood. In John 16:27, we understand that Jesus made us acceptable to God. There is no other way to the Father than through him. He is the foundation on which all life rests. Jesus became the first level so we can aspire to attain level 12. Therefore, level one, jasper, represents the blood of Jesus.

Attached to level one is level two, represented by sapphire. Blue brings restoration. Restoration comes after you have accepted Christ into your life. He restores you to your original spirit. You become a new creation. When considering your salvation, it looks like this: the blood of Jesus (level 1) restores you (level 2) so you begin to seek God's promises (level 3) for your life.

Level three is agate, which is a stone of many colors. It looks like a rainbow. A rainbow was sent by God as a promise to never flood the earth again. When you are saved and restored, the promises of God become available to you. You become eager to grow in the Word in both obedience to what he says and excitement to what he promises.

Level four is emerald. Emerald is green in color. It represents nature and life in its purest form. It's a transition from the filth of a sinful world to the beauty and harmony of your new life in Christ. The Christian is progressing in understanding as his nature changes, what he seeks changes, and what is beautiful to him changes. Here is what we know so far: the blood of Jesus (level1) brings restoration (level 2) to show us his promises (level 3) so we can become pure (level 4) in our thinking to include our needs, wants, and desires. God's promises not only help us achieve our desires, but they also protect us from the evil one and all of his schemes.

Level five is onyx. Onyx is black. It offers the power of God's protection. When you receive Christ and become his child by choice, God protects you from all evil. He sends angels out on your behalf. God, your Father, takes your life very seriously. Level six is carnelian. Carnelian is orange and brings joy! When you understand you're redeemed, restored, promises are yours, you are returning to your natural self, and you are protected, the joy of the Lord will overtake you. You should burst with love for the Lord and your fellow man. Your joy should overflow and help others see Christ in you.

The first six stones are what the Lord has done for you, his child, the believer in his. Jesus is all about you and wants you to be all about him. As we mature in love for Jesus, our hearts begin to seek him in every area of our life. Level seven, chrysolite, is a green apple color. It represents anointing oil. Level seven shifts the believer to asking the Lord for counsel, the Lord's desires, and seeking his kingdom. A believer begins to set aside earthly desires and becomes anointed for God's purpose.

Level eight, beryl, is light blue in color, representing the favor of God in your life. When our focus changes from "I" to, "your will, Lord," then the Lord brings favor in ways we never expected. He gives us favor so his message, love, will can be done. The favor of God is precious, and it brings blessings beyond comparison. Favor brings a new desire on the believer to become a God seeker.

The final four stones require a believer to trust God, truly call things out before they exist, decree, and believe. Level nine is topaz. Topaz is a mixture of gold, yellow, brown, and orange. It shimmers and changes colors. Topaz is full of heavenly intent and fire. The believer is seeking God intently and with fire. It's a desire to see God's will on earth as it is in heaven. The God seeker begins to call things out. Level ten is chrysoprase. Praise be to God! Chrysoprase is the most amazing pale green stone. It's the apple of God's eye. When a believer becomes the center of God's eye, the delight in that person is sincere. God can use them to move mountains. God is searching high and low for those who call out the promises and plans of his kingdom. Those mature believers are priceless.

Level eleven, jacinth, a fire red stone, burns in the heart of a mature God-fearing believer. This person is similar to Daniel. This believer will quiet lions and not bow to kings. This believer believes. There is no other way, purpose, God, or system. Jesus is the way, the truth, and the life. There is no other life outside of a life with God. Finally, level twelve is amethyst. Amethyst is purple. Purple symbolizes royalty. The believer is dressed in robes of heavenly purple, reigning forever with Christ and the Father in heaven. The top of the kingdom represents the glory, the Almighty. Jesus descended from level twelve to become level one so we can be one in him and one with God. God's final kingdom represents our earthly journey to our final place with him.

The meaning of each color:

1. Blood of Jesus
2. Restoration
3. Promises
4. Nature
5. Protection
6. Joy
7. Anointing
8. Favor
9. God Seeker
10. Call It Out
11. Mature Believer
12. Royalty

Now that we understand the levels and amazing characteristics of each stone, why would the Lord choose to give us this insight? I have taught this mystery to my group of ladies that I lead in Bible study, and as I was teaching this mystery, I began to ask God for understanding as to why he wanted me to know this. Yes, part of it is what we have to look forward to in heaven, but I believe like, everything else, the Lord wants what he shows us to be useful as we live on earth. The Lord's Prayer always tells us to remember, "on earth as it is in heaven." So, what about the Lord's kingdom can we bring to earth as it is in heaven? How do we use the Lord's characteristics of each stone to help us in everyday life?

Simultaneously during this study, the Lord taught me a great deal about the power of the decree. I learned that purposely decreeing God's Word into my life brought his promises for my life into reality. I also learned to be proactive in my life and choose the decrees I wanted. I was tired of waiting on the devil to tell me what to pray about. I decided it's my life and my decision on what I pray about. I learned how to target important things in my life and develop a battle plan to protect those things by decreeing God's promises into my life. The power of a decree changes everything.

By combining the Lord's teaching on the decree with the understanding of his kingdom colors, he helped me write the following understanding. This is a decree of who we are, what we have, and where our final resting place will be. It is a combination of Revelation from Scripture and revelation from the Holy Spirit. Promptings from the Holy Spirit of lessons learned throughout my entire life are present in this decree. I believe understanding it will change my life forever. This isn't a one-time read and place it on the shelf. This is a way of life. I believe this is a game changer. God has given us the keys to his kingdom through our Savior, Jesus Christ. He has provided a glimpse into our eternal kingdom dwelling and an understanding of what he has provided for us on earth. What do you want to believe? What do you want to lay claim to? What do you want to see working in your life? You get to choose. Your heart is the gate for the supernatural to flood the natural. Do you want to be ruined for normal, or do you just want the status quo? I believe God will give us all we ask him for. As you read the following decree from the levels of the colors, realize just how precise God is and how he doesn't leave anything out or undone. He isn't a God of confusion; he is a God of glory and revelation. But his secrets are only revealed to those who have a heart to find them. Get your heart ready to receive.

In Jesus's Name, We Decree:

We are bought and purchased with the highest of sacrifice, the blood of our Savior, Jesus Christ, the one and only Messiah, the one and only way to God; our firm foundation in which our feet never slip, our permanent home, our advocator, the one who holds the book of names. He is the beginning, the middle, and the end, the Lion of Judah and the Lamb who was slain, the only one pure enough to claim our restoration.

He is the restoration who calms my spirit and lays me down in still pastures, the restoration who removes my sins and replaces my life, and the one who baptizes me and forgets all my sins, who restores all my relationships and clothes me with his grace, and who calms my mind, heart, and soul. He lays out promises for my life to bring good and not evil, to give me hope and a future, to never leave or forsake me, to give me eternal life, to keep me and those I love free from sickness, danger, poverty, anguish, death, hell, and the grave, that strengthen my resolve and help me see my cause, and that move me into a pure relationship with him.

The love of my Savior washes me pure as snow and returns me to an unflawed, young spirit of unblemished posture, magnitude, pure love, and that all may eat from, one that bears kindness, peace, joy, love, gentleness, and trustworthiness, good fruit that blesses all who eat it, restored to our pure form before him so we may lift our eyes to him and find peace under his wings, our protector, our father, the one we have a relationship with.

God, our father, who art in heaven, hallowed be thy name. The Creator of this universe is our daddy, our protector, our strength. He is victory, justice, and vengeance; there is no other. He shall not be defeated. He is our protector, deliverer, judge, and eternal solitude. He never grows weary or turns his back on us. He sends our enemies running. He never backs down. He dresses us in his armor. He directs our paths. He places the weapons of warfare in our hands. He stands against all evil and commands his angels to protect us. He allows us to try his Word and give praise as he wins every battle. He fights for us while our hearts sing praise, for the joy of our Lord is our strength.

He wakes me up each morning with joy, and he holds my eyes and my head up. He gives me sunshine and nature for my enjoyment. His calm delight is the anchor for my soul. He delights in my prosperity, life, and victories. The joy of his love for me bubbles like a brook ever flowing, never-ending. He causes my spirit to laugh and brings relationships for my joy and pleasure. He brings music for my soul. When my soul cries and is in anguish, he brings a new day, a new hope, and a new memory. He won't leave me in a pit but turns beauty to ashes. He leaves no stone unturned, no tear unkept, and no laugh unused. His desire is for me to walk with him all the days of my life to return to him as a child, restore my soul to joy, and anoint my head with oil.

I'm anointed as Jesus was with precious oils that linger and bring favor. I am anointed to stand a part. I'm anointed for battle. I am separated from the turmoil of this world. It shall have no place in me. I anoint others with healing, peace, prosperity, and favor. I seek counsel from the Lord so that my actions represent him. My relationships are blessed by him. I am anointed to carry the Holy Spirit everywhere I go. I represent Jesus on this earth. Those who see me see something different, something they want.

I am marked with favor. All I touch prospers. My health, relationships, business, home, and teaching are marked with God's signet ring. I am favored to write decrees and speak them into the lives around me. God sees me and is pleased because I believe. I am capable of remaining humble and in awe of his power. I realize no good thing comes from me but through him. I can do the impossible. All things are possible for those you believe in him. I talk freely with others about his goodness and see through the eyes of the Holy Spirit with empathy, grace, and forgiveness. Although I sin, I repent, and God restores me. He resets the favor on my life and sends me out for him. He builds up my faith to help me seek him in all I do. He rewards my efforts and sparks my curiosity. He places a desire in my heart to seek him in new ways.

As my life surrounds his Word, as I cry out to become more like him, I become able to see. I become able to call things out. New mysteries, understandings, and questions fill my heart. I long to know him more to please him with my life. I long to see his promises in action, to seek his face and not his hand, to seek his presence, to understand my place, and to lead others to his fathership. I seek him in times of trouble. I praise him in times of victory, and I look for him in all situations and ask him to teach me, guide me, lead me, direct me, use me, fill me, and discipline me. In every situation, I acknowledge his Lordship and obey, no matter the cost. A God seeker moves when called without question. A God seeker handles high level callings and isn't afraid. A God seeker has wisdom beyond the natural, a true gift to bring heaven to earth, a gift to call out things of God and expect to see manifestation.

Call things that aren't as though they are. A studier is one who works my words into their hearts and lives by them, one who studies and spends time with me, one I can trust to represent my name well, one who is transparent and able to share life so all can see the goodness of God, one unafraid to be real, one who loves God in the purest of form who has their eyes on heavenly things, one who seeks first the kingdom of God, one who seeks to obey, seeks to work, and seeks to be generous, one who seeks to move as he directs, seeks to bring pleasure to the Lord, and seeks to walk out the goodness of God, and one God can trust and keep in the center of his eye.

One who is unified in cause, unified in love, and unified in purpose, one who sacrifices fully to the Creator, one who sacrifices their own needs and understanding for the sake of the world, one with an innocent heart, one who obeys without question, one willing to cut out all blemish to serve the Lord, one who God deeply favors, then so be it. Thy will be done. Use me, Lord, to carry out your work. One who God calls his very own, one who is loved deeply, never overlooked, kept in the center of his eye, Surrounded, guided, and protected, the one Jesus loves. One who seeks God in a way few do, one whose heart is tied to the Lord, is a representative worthy of wisdom beyond the natural and courage beyond fear.

Lord, our prayer is that we become mature believers you can depend on, believers who know you, believe in you, follow you, and defend you, believers who are surrounded inside and out by your Word, which moves in and through us, who do what your commission is: cleanse the lepers, heal the sick, cast out demons, and raise the dead; followers who tell everyone about your Son. Believers shine brightly for the cause of Christ, who do not shake in the storm, sleep in the garden, or run from the enemy, who have the wisdom to not be fooled, mature believers who lead others out of bondage and stare death in the face and not lose the fight. May you fill us with peace that surpasses all understanding, so we never question your love. Give us a spiritual hunger to see the face of Jesus.

Until we become royalty, and eternity brings our true identity, our real names, our non-sinful beings, may the Lord lead and guide us through this world. Until the time our spirits will live forever, may we seek after God every day. One day the robes of purple will replace the decay of this world. Our purpose from the beginning will be to meet our Father. This life and its words will pass away, and the **Word** will be visible. We will touch Scripture. We will live in the middle of his kingdom, something we could only imagine will now be reality. All the pain of a dying world will no longer be with us. Our Jesus will look us in the eye and say, "Well done, my good and faithful servant. Welcome home!"

We will walk on streets of gold, listen to heavenly music, and sit by the river of life. All who went before you will once again be alive to you. The pressure of a fallen system, the ugliness of Satan, and the smell of death are nowhere to be seen, heard, smelled, or touched. All worries will vanish. Day and night will disappear, nothing dirty will be allowed, and only those who belong to Jesus will be present. The tree of life will produce the fruit of life; with healing is in its leaves. Never again will anything be cursed. The shining of God, our Master, our Father, will be the only light we need.

Revelation 22:6–7: "Yes, I am on my way! Blessed be the one who keeps the words of the prophecy of this book."

Revelation 22:11: "Let the righteous maintain a straight course and the holy continue on in holiness."

Revelation 22:12–13:
Yes, I am on my way! I'll be there soon! I'm bringing my payroll with me. I'll pay all people for their full life's work. I'm A to Z, the First and the Final, the Beginning and Conclusion. How blessed are those who washed their robes! The Tree of Life is theirs for good, and they'll walk through the gates of the city. But outside for good are the cursed: sorcerers, fornicators, murders, idolaters—all who love and live lies. Rev. 22-20, I am on my way! I'll be there soon! The grace of Master Jesus be with all of you. Amen!

Endnotes

1. Martin Luther King Jr., *Strength to Love* (Minneapolis: Augsburg Fortress Publishing, 2010)
2. Hillsong United, Benjamin Hastings, Joel Houston, and Michael Fatkin, "So Will I (100 Billion Times)," recorded June 9, 2017, on *Wonder*, Sparrow Records and Capital Christian Music Group.
3. Hillsong United, "So Will I (100 Billion Times)."
4. *Webster's 1828 American Dictionary of the English Language*, Compact Edition (West Valley City, UT: Walking Lion Press, 2010).
5. Austin O Malley, *Keystones of Thought*, Fourth Edition (Greenwich: The Devin-Adair Company 1918).
6. "Hershel Walker Quotes," Brainy Quote.com, Brainy Media Inc. 2022, accessed October 14, 2022, https://www.brainy-quote.com/quotes/herschel_walker_131374.
7. Sarah O Brian, "Americans Spend Fifty-six Billion on Sporting Events," CNBC, September 11, 2017, 3:36 PM EDT.
8. *Rocky Balboa*, Sylvester Stallone (2006; Metro Goldwyn Mayer Pictures Revolution Studios, MGM Distribution Company and Sony Pictures), film.
9. *Jurassic Park*, directed by Steven Spielberg (1993; Universal Pictures Amblin Entertainment), film.
10. Patrick Rothfuss, *The Name of the Wind*, (New York: DAW Books, 2007).

11. Lana Vawser, *The Prophetic Voice of God: Learning to Recognize the Language of the Holy Spirit* (Shippensburg: Destiny Image Publishers, Inc., 2018).
12. James Clear, *Atomic Habits. How Long Does it Actually Take to Form a New Habit (Backed by Science)* (New York: Penguin Random House, 2018).
13. *Steele Magnolias*, directed by Herbert Ross (1989; Tri-Star Pictures), film.
14. American Soldier quote, no author. Found on *Me. Me.*, June 20, 2018.
15. *Greyhound*, Aaron Schneider (2020; Sony Pictures Entertainment), film.
16. Lana Vawser, *I Hear the Lord Say New Era* (Shippensburg, PA: Destiny Image Publishers, Inc., 2020).
17. Stephen Chbosky, *The Perks of Being a Wallflower* (New York: Pocket Books, 1999).
18. Cedella Marley and Cedella Marley Booker, *56 Thoughts from 56 Hope Road: The Sayings and Psalms of Bob Marley* (Newburyport: Hampton Roads Publishing Company, 2002).
19. Henry Ward Beecher, "Life Thoughts Gathered From the Extemporaneous Discourses of Henry Ward Beecher," *BiblioBazaar,* January 2010, 1858.
20. *A Boy Named Charlie Brown*, Bill Melendez (1969; Los Angeles, California; Cinema Center Films), Film.
21. Zig Ziglar and Julie Ziglar Norman, *Embrace the Struggle* (New York: Simon and Schuster, 2009).
22. Ronald Rook, *Daily Running Log* (New York: Penguin Random House, 2019).
23. Judah Smith, *How's Your Soul? Everything that matters starts with the inside you* (Nashville: Thomas Nelson, 2016).